THE WEALDWAY
AND THE
VANGUARD WAY

Wealdway commemoration marker post at Camp Hill, Ashdown Forest

THE WEALDWAY

and the

VANGUARD WAY

Kev Reynolds

CICERONE PRESS,
MILNTHORPE, CUMBRIA

ISBN 0902363 85 9
First Published 1987

Front cover:
Oasts and farm near Fordcombe, Wealdway.

All illustrations by the author.

Contents

River Medway in Tonbridge

Introduction

FROM Thames-side to clifftop, from suburbs to sea. In the Wealdway and the Vanguard Way we have two long-distance routes that traverse the country spreading south from London, and in so doing explore some of the finest landscapes in the south-east.

Contrary to the belief held by many, England's south-eastern corner is not one great urban sprawl broken only by a spaghetti-twist of motorways. Certainly there is a greater preponderance of concrete and brick here than one may expect to find in practically any other region of comparable size in Britain, but this is a view likely to cloud another reality. That reality is a more welcome one. It is one of magnificent broad vistas, a vast acreage of meadow and orchard, of hop garden and vineyard, of ancient parkland and high rolling heath, of woods alive with an extravagance of birdsong and mile upon mile of lovely downland, orchid-speckled and open to the sky. Along both Wealdway and Vanguard Way the walker experiences them all.

Those of us who live in the south and walk these footpaths know this truth, yet still there are surprises in store for us, too. Whilst out surveying the routes for this guide I found myself time and again walking for miles without coming across any habitation. On some days I went for several hours before finding a village large enough to boast even a single shop. More surprisingly, I was eight miles from the completion of the 80-mile Wealdway before I met another walker, even though there are many hundreds of miles of public footpath available for enjoyment, and thousands of ramblers living within easy access of them. I spied deer on several occasions - in woodland and out in the open. I sniffed out the habitat of fox and badger, saw a number of adders, was serenaded hourly by the glorious anthems of birdsong. Often I sprawled in the seething grasses to watch insects busying themselves on insect business, and delighted at butterflies tiptoeing across the delicate heads of numerous wild flowers that coloured the way. There was fragrance in the breeze and a peace broken only by nature's timeless rhythms. Walking in the countryside is, of course, more than simply putting one foot in front of the other. It is a way of absorbing that countryside and so enriching one's life. Walking the Wealdway or the Vanguard Way offers plenty of opportunities to do just that, in a series of landscapes that have been loved and tended through all the ages of man's occupation of these isles.

Both routes have much in common. Both begin in the bustle of towns and finish on breezy clifftop perches overlooking the English Channel. In between they cross the escarpment of the North Downs, enter the ever varied Weald, cross the great open heath of Ashdown Forest and march off to the marvellous barrier of the South Downs beyond which lies the sea. Long-distance walks that share a common aim, they touch or cross seven other lengthy 'Ways'; the Saxon Shore Way, London Countryway, North Downs Way and Pilgrims Way, the Greensand Way, Sussex Border Path and finally, the South Downs Way.

Forget the spaghetti-tangle of motorways, the wanderer in the south has a splendid network of footpaths that enable him to journey where no internal combustion engine can go. They lead to places of sheer enchantment, and if through the guidance of this book others are led to a discovery of the rich and colourful landscapes of the south-east, and in so doing are inspired to seek out more paths of enjoyment for a few hours or days of health-giving exercise, then this work has been fully justified.

Although considerably more stable than some other parts of Britain, this countryside is constantly changing and evolving. Even without man's efforts the landscapes of today will be slightly different tomorrow. That is the way it has always been, and how it ought to be. But bearing this in mind it is to be hoped that the descriptions of the routes contained in this guide will be sufficiently clear for some years to enable walkers to follow the way without too much difficulty. However, modern farming practices sometimes mean that woodlands are thinned or clear-felled, hedgerows altered and isolated trees that today form a strategic landmark may well disappear tomorrow. In some cases stiles may be replaced by gates, or vice-versa. Should you find that a section of your route has been seriously altered for some reason or other, perhaps you'd be good enough to let me know by dropping a note c/o the publisher of this book, and I'll check it out for any subsequent edition.

In the meantime it is my fervent hope that you will gain as much pleasure from walking the Wealdway and/or the Vanguard Way as I have done. Please respect the life of the countryside and those who work and live in it. The Country Code is a guide to remember, but it merely follows in the wake of principles set by Octavia Hill, a champion of the countryside and one of the founders of the National Trust, who wrote at the turn of the century:

'Let the grass growing for hay be respected, let the primrose roots be left in their loveliness in the hedges, the birds unmolested and the gates shut. If those who frequented country places would consider those who live there, they would better deserve, and more often retain, the rights and privileges they enjoy.'

Kev Reynolds

The Wealdway heads through this tunnel of trees near Nash Street

A Stroll Down to the Sea

TWO routes with a common aim, the Wealdway and the Vanguard Way set out to walk to the sea. The first begins in Gravesend on the edge of the Thames east of London, and measures 82 miles on its way to Beachy Head outside Eastbourne. In truth, the *official* line starts on the outskirts of Gravesend and stops short of Beachy Head's plunging cliffs, but most walkers, I feel sure, would find it more satisfactory to link the river with the sea, and so for the sake of a couple of extra miles this seems the most appropriate route for this guidebook.

Unlike the Vanguard Way, the Wealdway has the advantage of frequent waymarking with a distinctive WW on a yellow arrow, which in no way detracts from the pleasures of the journey, but rather gives reassurance now and then that you're still on route. There is a problem, however, in the spacing of accommodation. Whereas the Vanguard Way conveniently links villages that have Youth Hostels, and one town with hotel and bed and breakfast accommodation, the Wealdway is somewhat spartan in this respect and as a consequence requires one or two stages to be a little longer perhaps than some walkers might wish, in its efforts to find lodging along the way. A judicious study of accommodation lists in the future may ease the situation, while those who are particularly attracted to long-distance walks will not find the length of any of these sections especially daunting. One way of overcoming any fear on this score, of course, is to nibble at the route with the use of motor transport - one car at either end of the day stage - and tackle the walk on occasional weekends, for example, rather than in one continuous outing.

The Vanguard Way sets out from East Croydon and works its way with much interest through a corner of Surrey, into Kent and then for the most part in Sussex to finish on that lovely belvedere of Seaford Head, not far from Cuckmere Haven and the Seven Sisters. This is a route of 62 miles that could easily be completed in a five-day holiday. Hitch a couple of days onto a bank holiday weekend, and a very pleasant outing may be achieved. On the other hand, should the idea be to walk a stage now and then, the Vanguard Way is a little easier than the Wealdway to arrange in this manner. Public transport is, at present, more readily available along the line of this route, while a car-assisted walk is quite a practical proposition.

Ever-Varied Landscapes

THE GEOGRAPHY of the south-east, as experienced on these two walks, is dominated by the Weald of Kent and Sussex, that great expanse of country named Anderida by the Romans. Long, long ago all this land was covered by the Jurassic Sea, and when it gradually disappeared rivers flowed from Britain's highland regions bringing with them coarse-grained sediments that emptied into a vast fresh-water lake. In the bed of this lake there accumulated deposits of clay and sand, and over countless dark centuries more deposits were laid by inrushing seas and later, sediments containing miniscule sea shells. On the beds of clay there formed a layer of chalk created by these sea shells. A layer 1,000 feet thick.

Violent movements of the earth forced the rocks upward into a long dome formation, and then began the work of erosion. Rivers, and weathering by rain, wind and frost, gradually removed the chalk cover from the central portion of this great dome, and began to set to work on the lower portion of clays and sands exposed, with the edges of the dome remaining to form natural boundaries.

The chalk edges are the Downs we see today. The clay and sand central area being the Weald. This is the foundation of the landscapes through which we journey.

The Weald today houses the 'Garden of England'. To walk either of these routes in springtime is to experience the glory of a countryside in bloom. Both routes lead through orchards and their blossoms can create heady memories of lavish colouring, fragrance and promise. The Wealden clay, so different from the chalk of the Downs, supports a broad-based agriculture. You'll come across meadowlands of grazing sheep; wheatfields and fields of cabbages; fruit orchards and vineyards; woodlands of beech and oak in whose glades primroses, wood anemones and bluebells offer gifts of the season; as well as plantations of pine, dark and mysterious beyond the tunnel of your path, where you may be sure nature has found a sanctuary for timid creatures.

When the Romans knew it, the Weald was a great forest stretching for some ninety miles. Nowadays the forest has gone; cleared for agriculture, for settlements, for the firing of the iron-making furnaces that made this part of the country a major centre of industrial power from before the Romans, until the 18th century; and cleared too for the building of men-o'-war when Britain's navy ruled the waves.

Although the forest cover has all but gone from the Weald, there are innumerable woods of varying sizes. Among some of them lie still waters that once were hammer ponds in the days of the iron industry. Strangely quiet, tranquil sheets of water they are today, but for centuries they provided the energy to drive the pounding hammers that symbolise this once-important industry. They, and the magnificent manor houses that were built on the proceeds of iron-making, are all that remain today.

The North Downs have been carved into a dramatic escarpment that does not become fully apparent until the path suddenly comes to the lip of hillside and the world falls away at your feet. The South Downs, however, roll in a line of broad-backed hills; from their summits great spaces appear on all sides, the Weald to the north, the sea to the south. The North Downs form a wall of green that holds London from swelling into the Weald; the South Downs manage to keep the surging tides of the Channel where they belong.

As for Ashdown Forest, this makes an admirable halfway point for both routes. Basically the Forest is no longer forest, but rather a high open region of heathland comprising about 6,000 acres in all, dotted here and there by stands of pine known as 'clumps' that are thought to derive from hideouts used by hunting parties waiting to bag themselves deer. In some parts of the Forest it is possible on a clear day to see both North and South Downs forming the limits of each horizon.

Of the many waterways that drain this southern country, only the Medway and Cuckmere are rivers of any consequence. Both routes accompany each of the rivers for short distances; the Wealdway experiencing the Medway as a calm, yet broad stretch of navigable water, while the Vanguard Way has the better part of the Cuckmere where it anxiously winds toward the freedom of the sea, whereas the Wealdway traces its placid course through meadows and along willow-lined banks of quiet charm. The Medway is the river of the Weald; the Cuckmere, the river that breaches the South Downs.

Wandering through History

PROBABLY no other region of Britain has a closer association with the various stages of man's development of these isles. Probably no other region of Britain has been so consistently moulded by the passage of history, nor suffered forces of invasion more often. Perhaps this is not surprising, for a glance at a map will show immediately the ease of continental access. Of course, when the Downs were formed, Kent was joined to continental Europe by a landbridge, and the Channel is only a comparatively recent separation that has been no great deterrent to the ambitions of land-hungry invaders.

Early on came Belgic tribes who brought with them skills unknown by the native Celts. In the New Stone Age our Neolithic ancestors left evidence of their presence in the form of burial chambers and cause-wayed camps. The Wealdway passes beside the Coldrum Stones, just below the North Downs, where 22 skeletons have been discovered in the remains of a long barrow, and on Combe Hill above Jevington on the South Downs, broken pieces of pottery have been found and identified as belonging to the civilisation that occupied this splendid viewpoint some four and a half thousand years ago, while on Dry Hill, the Vanguard Way crosses the site of an Iron Age encampment comprising twenty-four acres.

It was Caesar who, in 55 BC, said that Kent was 'the most civilised part of Britain', but it was the later occupation under Claudius that began in AD 42, that set in motion Rome's far greater civilising processes. Both Wealdway and Vanguard Way follow for a while the route of the ancient London to Lewes road that was created to service Roman iron foundries in the Weald, and not far away from the Wealdway on Camp Hill, Ashdown Forest, traces of the *agger* on either side of the old road can clearly be seen. A little farther south, near Fairwarp, great deposits of slag and ash dating from the period of Roman occupation, show that even then this corner of the country was used by them as a major site for smelting iron.

The influence of Rome is all over the south-east, and both our routes have plenty of opportunities to explore corners that bear that influence in one way or another. There was a Roman villa in Titsey Park on the Vanguard Way, and much farther south, deep in the Sussex countryside, the same route crosses near Limekiln Farm the site of an agricultural estate laid out by the Romans some sixteen hundred years ago, and the map shows a neat pattern of tracks and roadways equally spaced in a form of grid - measuring the five *actus* unit favoured by clear Roman minds.

After the Romans, England's south was ruled by a succession of Saxons; Kent had kingdoms ruled by Jutes, Sussex by South Saxons. Each county developed independently in custom, law and religion. When St. Augustine arrived at Pegwell Bay in AD 597, he and his forty monks brought Christianity to Kent, while Sussex was not converted for another hundred years. Saxon churches are, perhaps, few and far between on our routes, but at Arlington and Jevington on the South Downs there are two examples, and at Bidborough the Wealdway passes beside the lovely old church that dates back a thousand years while Luddesdown Court on the North Downs, although not strictly Saxon, is said to have been created by Saxon builders under the management of Norman overseers. It has been occupied continuously for some 900 years, since the days when Odo, Bishop of Bayeux, came over with the Conqueror and set up home here.

The Norman invasion of 1066 brought a great bout of development to the south-east; most noticeably in the powerful construction of castles and solid-looking churches, of which there are fine examples to be admired in many towns and villages. The Norman remains of Tonbridge Castle can clearly be seen beside the Medway on the Wealdway's route, while the Vanguard Way skirts the boundary of the site of Starborough Castle near Edenbridge, and not far from Alfriston the route passes close to the splendid Charleston Manor, begun within twenty years of the Norman conquest.

There are many other fine manor houses, yeoman's houses and small country cottages that have stood for centuries to grace the byways of our land, and beside which our routes work their interesting, ever-varied ways. The Middle Ages left a heritage of architectural splendour that we can enjoy to this day; Horselunges Manor near Hellingly represents one such building that makes the passing rambler pause for a moment to wonder at the past. Old Dairy Farm in a quiet lane in Crockham Hill is another. There are lovely little cottages tucked among leafy bowers at Bullingstone. And there is the ruined priory near Upper Dicker that has seen so many changes since it was founded in 1229; Michelham Priory on the path of the Wealdway.

Through the Weald there are a number of sunken lanes and pathways developed from the passage of heavy horse-drawn waggons transporting iron-ore hundreds of years ago. There are also old quarries, now green with moss and overhung by trees, that tell of past use in providing stone for building or for the laying of roads, or for iron-stone in the production of cannon and railings and ornamental gates.

Along both Wealdway and the Vanguard Way history is laid out for the unravelling. The paths themselves that combine to create these long-distance routes are in many instances the same paths that have been used as country ways by country dwellers for centuries. Some lead through farmways and beside private houses, and even through neat gardens on an historical errand. They are as important to our heritage as are the farms and villages they connect, and they form a mile-by-mile link with the past so that we are, indeed, wandering through history.

Tonbridge Castle - the Wealdway leads between this and the Medway

On Nature's Trail

WITH the wide variety of landscapes to be enjoyed along both routes contained in this guide, and with the diversity of soil types experienced along the way, the walker will find a wealth of wild flowers to brighten the miles. Since the Downs are predominantly chalk-based with a cropped grassland cover, there is a certain mineral deficiency that precludes a number of common plants from being found here. However, there is a magnificent variety of flowers that actually thrive on this type of soil, and of these the orchid is the most extravagant. There are several different species that vary in quantity from one year to the next. The Common Spotted and Fragrant Orchid are often found together, sometimes in massed congregations, while the Lady Orchid is a rarity and, in company with the Musk and Man Orchid, can only be found now in this corner of the country.

In addition to orchids there are masses of cowslips on the Downs, their pendulous heads swaying in the breeze. There's Kidney Vetch and Wild Thyme and Yellow-wort. Towards the end of summer Autumn Gentians appear, while Old Man's Beard clambers over bushes wherever there is chalky soil.

Along the banks of the Medway comfrey is found growing. Beside other streams and small rivers it's quite possible that you will see clumps of Yellow Iris, or Himalayan Balsam and Hemp Agrimony with butterflies drawn to its pink flower heads. In clear stretches no doubt you'll come across Marsh Marigold, Waterlily and Water Mint.

In springtime the woods are awash with bluebells, and one of the walker's most pleasant memories can come from strolling for mile upon mile among magnificent beeches with acres of bluebells turning the ground to a woodsmoke haze of colour. Primroses are a feature in some areas; wood anemones in others, daffodils elsewhere.

On Ashdown Forest bracken and gorse grow everywhere, but there's also broom, very similar to gorse but without the spikes, and growing low against the ground are bilberries whose fruit is sweet and juicy to eat in summer. There are boggy stretches where moisture oozes from the acid soil, and here there are various mosses and sedges and little patches of cotton grass now and then.

Birdlife will brighten any walk. Woodpeckers are often heard drumming away in the woods, and you'll often be startled by 'the policeman of the woods', the jay, as he shrieks a warning to fellow inhabitants that you're on your way. There'll no doubt be pheasants exploding from your feet as you wander along a hedgerow. There'll be all sorts of nests hidden in them, too. There'll be jackdaws circling above the woods and maybe a stonechat or two flitting nervously from one gorse bush to another as you stride across Ashdown Forest.

There are ducks along the rivers. Perhaps you'll be fortunate enough to catch a glimpse of a kingfisher skimming above the water - you're sure to see dragonflies darting to and fro indecisively almost wherever there's water, and no doubt you'll see swans, not only along the Medway and Cuckmere, but perhaps nesting in a quiet inland stream. Should you spy one sitting on a nest, leave well alone. On the Downs you'll be serenaded by skylarks. In morning and evening time the woods will be orchestrated to full pitch by the massed choirs of the air. Birdsong is a gift to treasure.

On Nature's Trail it doesn't really matter whether you recognise particular flowers or birds by name, so long as they bring enjoyment to your day. They will accompany any walk, adding colour, fragrance or sound. You may well spy deer. There will be plenty of rabbits and hares; perhaps a fox or two. You may well come across an adder. Step carefully aside; it'll do no harm so long as it doesn't feel threatened. There may be lizards sunning themselves over the heathland of the Forest. Keep an eye open for them; they're characters in your landscape of wonder.

If you wander through the countryside without haste, with your eyes and ears alert, sniffing the breezes and stepping lightly, the world of nature becomes part of you, and you a part of nature's world. If you walk in the company of a friend, or friends, save your conversations for moments of rest, or you'll miss the creatures with whom you share the countryside. Be observant and absorb all that the countryside can offer, then the experience of the Wealdway and the Vanguard Way will be elevated to a higher plain that will enrich the days ahead with a kaleidoscope of memories.

It's a lovely world; don't take it for granted.

Transport and Accommodation

PUBLIC transport in rural areas becomes scarcer with each passing year. It is therefore inadvisable to quote present day service details for bus routes that may well be out-of-date before this guide even goes into print. However, a brief listing of villages and towns along the way that have some bus and/or train link is quoted at the end of each section's route descriptions. Walkers who may wish to use public transport are strongly advised to contact the offices of those operators and obtain precise details of specific services as required. Addresses will be found at the back of this book.

Accommodation details are also only briefly given. Where a town or village en route has hotel or bed and breakfast accommodation at present a note is made. Again, as with public transport, changes occur with some regularity. You are strongly advised to consult the latest edition of the Ramblers' Association *Bed and Breakfast Guide,* which I have found invaluable. In addition, the South-East England Tourist Board supplies information in two useful 'Where to Stay' publications: *Hotels, Motels and Guest Houses* and *Farmhouses, Bed and Breakfast, Inns and Hostels.*

Where Youth Hostels are conveniently situated along the routes, full information is given as to location, facilities available etc. Membership of YHA can be arranged by writing to the National Office, whose address is given at the back of this book, or in emergency at the hostel itself. Up-to-date details of opening dates and times, as well as current prices, will be found in the YHA Guide. This is obtainable through W.H.Smith's outlets, or free with membership.

Equipment for the Walks

NO SPECIALISED equipment will be required for either route. Ramblers will be aware of the need for comfortable, easy-fitting boots or stout shoes. Boots are preferable, especially when negotiating muddy sections! Shorts will be comfortable wear on many stages at certain times of the year, although sometimes nettles or brambles tend to reach onto the path, and then leg protection will be needed. In our unsettled climate no walker will set out for five or six days or so without carrying waterproofs. Waterproof overtrousers are often handy for the crossing of hayfields after rain, or early in the morning with the dew still fresh.

A light rucksack should be sufficient to carry spare clothing, waterproofs and overnight toilet items. In addition a small first aid kit should be carried, plus food for the day. While there are pubs that serve food scattered along both routes, it is not always the right time of day when you reach them. So take a packed lunch with you.

Vanguard Way crosses a stream in the Ashdown Forest

Using the Guide

THE MAPS included in this guide should be sufficient to meet your mile-by-mile requirements. However, at the head of each section a note is given on the specific Ordnance Survey sheet covering the area described. The 1:50,000 scale (1¼ inches = 1 mile) will give an adequate overall picture of the route's progress. A grid reference is quoted here and there to enable you to locate your exact position with some ease.

Throughout the guide I have sought to give additional information on particularly interesting places and features seen along the way. In the text these are marked with a cross reference number, and information is outlined at the end of each section corresponding with this text number.

In these days of competitive and record breaking walks there is a tendency for many to rush through the countryside with one eye on the clock and no time for the more leisurely pleasures to be enjoyed on the way. As an antedote to this attitude I have specifically written this guide with a more relaxed outlook, and attempted to bring out the flavour of these walks by including a few brief anecdotal snippets. My own experience of walking the Wealdway and the Vanguard Way may not be particularly remarkable, other than in witnessing the extraordinary nature of the ordinary common scenes and pleasures of the countryside. But it is to be hoped that the notes given here may enliven the text and inspire others who follow to absorb as much of the landscapes and the creatures that people it, as possible.

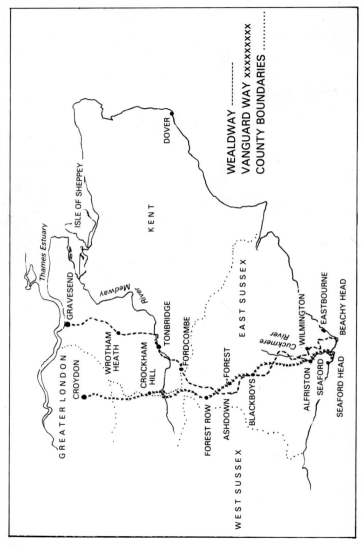

WEALDWAY ----------
VANGUARD WAY xxxxxxxxxx
COUNTY BOUNDARIES ....

First sight of Luddesdown on the North Downs

The Wealdway

Background

THE IDEA of a long-distance route for walkers through the Weald of Kent and Sussex, linking the River Thames with the English Channel, was first put forward in 1970 by members of the Ramblers' Association. The concept, however, was easier to consider than to effect, for although there were many existing rights of way that could be joined into one continuous path, there were considerable difficulties encountered in the southern section between Uckfield and the sea. On top of these difficulties, a major motorway building programme was under way in Kent, south of Gravesend, cutting across the line of the proposed route, and there was also the construction of the Tonbridge Flood Relief Barrier on the Medway near Haysden. Together these combined to create innumerable headaches of planning for the Wealdway Steering Group.

That the Wealdway was completed, and opened in September 1981 in a ceremony at Camp Hill on Ashdown Forest, is a triumph of patience and persistence for the Group.

The Route

BEACHY HEAD lies almost due south of Gravesend, and if you draw a straight line on a map from one to the other you'll see that it passes through some rather fine patches of country. Footpaths, of course, rarely follow straight lines, which is perhaps just as well. By linking existing rights of way the line inevitably becomes a meandering one, and since it winds its way to and fro across the map, so it becomes possible to include certain areas that otherwise would be by-passed. Ashdown Forest, for example, is a region well worth exploring. So the route grows until a pattern emerges.

On leaving Gravesend the Wealdway immediately heads across a fairly level stretch of farmland, goes through woodlands and into the folding vales that mark the 'hinterland' of the North Downs around the charming little hamlet of Luddesdown. Soon after, having roamed into more woodlands, it reaches the lip of the North Downs escarpment where the Weald is laid out as a broad canvas below. Down there, across the ancient track of the Pilgrims Way, there stand the Neolithic stones of the Coldrum Long Barrow on the outskirts of Trottiscliffe.

Continuing, the way goes through yet more woodlands and over meadows; under the monstrous roar of the M20 motorway and into the peace of a green countryside again. There are little villages, then the extensive tree cover of Mereworth Woods where forest tracks draw the walker to another fine vantage point at Gover Hill whose vast panorama looks into the real Garden of England.

There are orchards to wander through. The splendid setting of West Peckham; once more meadows and orchards again; acre upon acre of fruit trees that make you reel with wonder when the blossoms are out. It's a landscape of delight, dotted here and there with white-cowled oast houses and lovely old farms. And then, the Medway. Four miles of towpath bring the walker into the best parts of Tonbridge, leading beside the remains of the huge walls of its castle, before plunging once more into the rich green solitude of the countryside. The Medway's banks are traded for higher ground and the marvellous ridge on which sits Bidborough, a village with an ancient church and a broad view at every door.

Dodging up and down steep hillsides, exploring intimate little valleys, the Wealdway goes through Speldhurst, past several idyllic cottages and into magical woodland with a clear stream conjuring fairy tales from childhood days. And then to Fordcombe where you feel a change is imminent. That change comes subtly. You've become accustomed to broad views and meadows, but south of Fordcombe the views and meadows have a different quality of light, and just beyond Stone Cross one of the loveliest valleys on the whole route entices with immense charm. Hills and valleys, meadows and woodlands laid out as if by the hand of a landscape artist.

Sussex takes over from Kent. The route follows a clear stream to the edge of Withyham. A long driveway takes you into another land of wide vistas, then to Five Hundred Acre Wood - straight out of A.A.Milne - whose path through was dedicated by the landowner as a right of way in 1970 in recognition of European Conservation Year. There are some magnificent beeches in this wood, full of power and authority, but the nature of the route suddenly changes as the way emerges onto the high open heathland of Ashdown Forest; all gorse and bracken and stands of pine. And yet more broad vistas.

From the open landscapes of the Forest the way drops into more woods and agricultural country once again. Here was once the heart of England's iron-making. Now it lies peaceful and serene. Birds sing where hammers once pounded and furnaces roared. The air smells of fresh-cut grass, not smoke and smelting.

Then through the trim grassland of Buxted Park with its stately trees and immaculate shrubs, dropping down to the little River Uck that leads to Hempstead Mill. Up and down more hillsides, along a lane, through meadows again and beside Tickerage Mill to reach the village of Blackboys. From here the way dives immediately into fine country again, past the landscaped gardens of New Place, whose gentle waterfalls cascade with a song and a dash of spray, before heading across a large area of fields and meadows and woodlands that bring you to East Hoathly.

Not far away stands the village of Chiddingly, and a meeting of the Vanguard Way. Three more miles of interest lead to Hellingly, whose lovely church is set in a circular churchyard lined with neat cottages. A superb situation. Outside the hamlet the Wealdway goes through the grounds and beside the moat of the impressive 15th century timbered Horselunges Manor.

At Horsebridge the Wealdway has recently been subjected to a slight re-routing because of a small housing development, but it quickly returns to countryside once more, and by way of a series of fields to historic Michelham Priory. The South Downs are drawing near, and out of Upper Dicker they loom blue and inviting on the horizon. A pleasant stroll alongside the silver waters of the Cuckmere is exchanged for more fields that lead to Arlington. There's a reservoir nearby that entices a varied collection of wildfowl, but the wanderer following the Wealdway is likely to be more attracted by the beckoning hills than a deviation at this stage, and before long Wilmington is reached. This village has a splendid street, a lovely old church, the remains of a Priory - and the huge chalk figure of The Long Man etched on the wall of the Downs behind it. The Wealdway leads directly to its feet.

There follows a traversing path along the edge of the Downs with enormous views stretched below and out to the north. With cowslips at your boots and larks singing above, it is truly a walk in the sky. The downland path leads to Folkington, and from Folkington to Jevington. Jevington inhabits a tight valley surrounded by the Downs. The route climbs steeply to reach Combe Hill; an ancient belvedere with a history thousands of years old. Another foothold in the sky.

A walk along a broad ridge, with views now off to the nearby sea, and with Eastbourne directly below, brings the route to Willingdon Hill. More fine views, of distant plain and nearby vale and the sea glistening in the south. In no time at all the world falls away at your feet and the Wealdway's journey is over.

Beachy Head, where the tides of the Channel swirl far below. It's a worthy end to a delightful walk.

SECTION 1: GRAVESEND TO WROTHAM HEATH

Distance: 13½ miles

Maps: O.S. Landranger series; Sheets 177 *East London Area* and 188 *Maidstone and the Weald of Kent* 1:50,000

Accommodation: Gravesend - Hotels and b&b
Wrotham Heath - Hotel
Elsewhere - b&b in Addington (1½ miles N.E. of Wrotham Heath). Youth Hostel in Kemsing (5 miles west of Wrotham Heath; bus to Seal, then 1 mile walk).

As has already been explained, the Wealdway officially begins on the outskirts of Gravesend. However, for those who would prefer to walk from the edge of the Thames, this guide starts in Gravesend itself and adds two miles to the official first stage distance of 11½ miles.

Once out of town the Wealdway is soon marching across fields and through woodlands onto the backbone of the North Downs. It explores a series of lovely valleys around the tiny village of Luddesdown, recently saved from the threat of being taken over by the Defence Ministry as a tank training ground. Then more woodlands to the lip of the Downs, and a steep descent into the Weald at the Neolithic burial chamber of the Coldrum Stones near Trottiscliffe. A few more fields with expansive views, then under the M20 motorway before plunging once more into pleasant countryside on the approach to Wrotham Heath.

For the purposes of this guide, then, the Wealdway begins on the banks of the Thames where the Tilbury Ferry discharges its passengers from Essex. Here also begins the Saxon Shore Way.(1)

Facing the town of Gravesend(2) turn left and walk along West Street. In a few yards you'll see Town Pier on your left and opposite, on the right-hand side of the road, the inauspicious start of the High Street. Go up High Street, which is now a pedestrian precinct, to reach King Street which crosses it. This street is full of the bustle associated with a main shopping thoroughfare, which of course it is. A rucksack seems rather out of place here! Cross King Street into Windmill Street and follow along this as far as the Civic Centre. Now bear right to enter Wrotham Road, the A227, where it emerges from Stone Street. Continue along Wrotham Road all the way out of town until it approaches the main A2. On reaching a roundabout continue straight ahead and under the road bridge, there to take the footpath

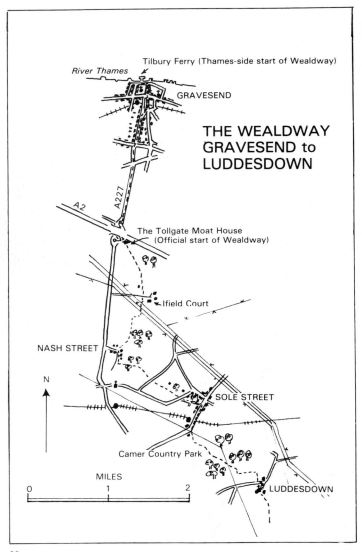

The Tilbury Ferry at Gravesend where the Wealdway begins by the Thames

immediately on the left and cross with care two side roads to pass in front of the Tollgate Moat House. (Car parking to the side of it.) About 50 yards beyond the Moat House the Wealdway proper begins at a stile on the right.

Go over the stile to enter the grounds of the Moat House between the boundary fence and motel buildings. A few yards along this, a gate on the left leads into a field with a finger post pointing to Ifield. Cross the large field diagonally half-right towards a line of willow trees. On reaching a broad farm track running along the edge of the field, turn right and follow it. Maintaining this direction you will soon come before the 18th century farmhouse of Ifield Court. Here turn right, and almost immediately break away to the left along the edge of another field to pass beneath power lines. There are orchards on the left. When these end the track turns right, then bears left after a short distance. It later becomes little more than a path beside woods, then is enclosed by trees until joining a metalled road in the hamlet of Nash Street, which consists of a handful of neat cottages. Turn left to follow this road.

After about 200 yards you'll come to a gate in the field ahead and see Nurstead Church across the fields. Turning away from this you'll see to the left of the gate a stile with a Wealdway marker. Take the path beyond the stile through a tunnel of trees, which is most attractive, down a slope to two more stiles. After the second of these keep to the left-hand edge of a large field and continue along it until the path brings you onto a quiet road. Cross over the road, still following a footpath that leads in about 500 yards to a stile in the fence on the left. Go diagonally half-right across this small field with a barn seen off to the left, and come out onto another road. Turn right. Twenty yards down the road a path on the left leads through woods, along the edge of a row of bungalow gardens, and meets a junction with a crossing path. Turn left and come onto Manor Road; a residential street.

Walk along Manor Road until it meets the main B2009 road. This is the heart of the village of Sole Street. There's a shop opposite, and on the left of the junction a 16th century Yeoman's House in the ownership of the National Trust.

Turn right and walk along the B2009, coming shortly to the railway station and Railway Inn, which serves snacks for those already in need of refreshment. Continue along the road for a further 250 yards. Here the road bears to the right. On the left is the entrance to Camer Country Park,(3) and immediately on the left of the Park entrance runs a wide track. Walk along this with the Park seen over the hedge on your right. After a while the way deserts the Park boundary and skirts off to the left, eventually passing a cottage. Keep on the track as it traces the right-hand edge of a large field with a wood on the right. When the wood ends, the Wealdway is crossed (unseen) by the route of the London Countryway.(4) Continue ahead, now with woods on the left, to pass beneath power lines and enter the woods at the left-hand corner of the field. The path in the trees rapidly brings you to a stile at the edge of a field. Over the stile turn right and go down the slope to find a second stile halfway down. Head off to the left, following the fence and line of trees with some interesting views opening ahead.

Apart from the power lines which intrude with their stark, ugly contempt for the countryside they inhabit, this is a corner of great beauty. The valley falling away, the rolling hills with their clusters of broad leaved trees and the marching hedgerows, all combine to create a scene of quiet charm. This is an England that time has moulded with care. It is a pleasure to wander slowly through it, pacing history, sensing tranquility. The few buildings that can be seen below are part of the hamlet of Luddesdown.

Continue along the hillside, cross a wire fence by way of a stile and keep straight ahead until you see a footpath descending the slope to the right. Go down this, across the field to the right of the buildings ahead - Luddesdown Village Hall. The path brings you onto a lane at a road junction. The proper route crosses the lane and goes round to the churchyard, but it's only a few strides to take the road opposite leading towards the entrance to Luddesdown Church.(5)

Go past the churchyard with its wall on your right. Now walk ahead through the farmyard, keeping a barn on your right, and find a stile in the fence to your left. Enter the field and wander up the slope. Halfway up the slope take a moment to look back at the setting of Luddesdown and its huddle of church, farm buildings and houses, with its sweep of valley and clusters of trees, and try to imagine how it might have been when Odo, Bishop of Bayeux, lived here nine hundred years ago. It could hardly have been much smaller then!

On reaching a gate near the top of the slope go through into the next field and follow along its right-hand edge with its boundary of trees. At the top of the field the trees begin to descend the slope ahead. Where they end there is a stile, and the path cuts across the field to meet it. Beyond this is a large field in a delightful valley known as the Bowling Alley. The Wealdway cuts right through it.

I sat on the edge of the field for a few minutes to absorb the countryside about me. All was peaceful save for the call of jackdaws lazily circling over the woods. The valley certainly was attractive. It swept away from me in a wash of gold - oil seed rape. It was barred by the deep greenery of oak and beech beyond with a house or two peeping out of the exuberant June growth. There was a sense of mystery in the tree crowded horizon that I was in no hurry to unravel, but when I set off again the path took me waist deep through the rape, and as I emerged on the far side I found my legs had turned yellow from the pollen.

The path which leads through the Bowling Alley goes straight ahead to reach a quiet country road. Turn right, then along the right fork a few yards later. Down the slope you come shortly to the attractive oast roundel and cottage of Great Buckland Farm. This is all delightful back-of-beyond country. Passing the farm on your right continue along the road uphill for almost 200 yards. On the left you'll come to a gate and a stile. Cross this stile and follow the footpath ahead, past the end of a wood, then between fences going uphill before entering the woodland. The path eventually brings you out to a field which you must cross diagonally half-right towards a large beech tree. Then turn

31

Great Buckland Farm near Luddesdown on the Wealdway

left and follow along the edge of the field to reach a track in the corner. This track is a bridle path which is sometimes rather muddy. Continue along this track with a fence on your right, to reach a road. (A farm driveway is reached before this road, with access to it; ignore this and continue along the track until you reach the road proper.)

Turn left on the road, and in a few yards pass the entrance to Boughurst Street Farm on your left. About 300 yards beyond the farm the road bends to the right. Straight ahead you will see a gateway. Enter the field and keep to its left-hand boundary to find a stile on your left. Cross this and turn immediately to the right through this field, then straight on as far as a farm with a stile leading onto a road. (Grid ref: 655624) Head right for about 30 yards, then take the path on your left which enters Whitehorse Wood. The route is clear throughout this wood, with waymarks where crosstracks occur. After little over half a mile the path comes out of the woods on the very lip of the North Downs with a hint of space beyond. With full foliage in the trees and hedges the great expanse of the panorama is broken into fragments of views, but the impression gained is one of a vast plain spread out below; the Weald.

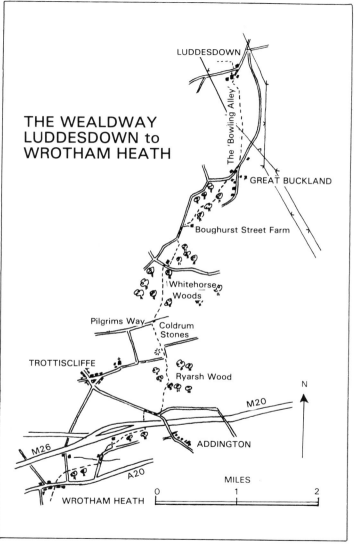

THE WEALDWAY
LUDDESDOWN to
WROTHAM HEATH

LUDDESDOWN

The 'Bowling Alley'

GREAT BUCKLAND

Boughurst Street Farm

Whitehorse Woods

Pilgrims Way

Coldrum Stones

TROTTISCLIFFE

Ryarsh Wood

M20

N

M26

ADDINGTON

A20

MILES

0   1   2

WROTHAM HEATH

The Neolithic Coldrum Stones below the North Downs

The path, banked by hedges, descends the steep slope of the Downs. In damp conditions this path can be rather slippery, so beware. At the foot of the slope a few steps lead onto the Pilgrims Way,(6) which at this point coincides with the North Downs Way.(7) Turn right and walk along it for a few yards to reach a lane. Here on the left is a sign to the Coldrum Long Barrow. Take the path indicated, alongside a large field with a view of the North Downs stretching off to the east beyond the Medway gap. The path comes to a farm access road. Continue straight ahead to find the Coldrum Stones(8) on your right.

Passing the Coldrum Stones on your right, continue along the farm road until it curves to the right. Leave it and go straight ahead on a track towards woods, which you enter on the right. There is a yellow Wealdway marker on a tree, but you must keep an eye open for it. It indicates the point at which to enter the wood. Go through Ryarsh Wood to emerge in a field corner. Bear left along the edge of the wood, over two stiles and to the right of a shed onto a road. Turn right and wander along this road until you see the entrance to a quarry on the left.

Note: *If you plan to spend the night in Addington, turn left along the road. This will lead over the motorway and into the village half a mile away.*

Cross the road to the quarry - a great sand pit. Immediately to the right of the quarry boundary fence you will find a path. Follow this. It takes you under the motorway (M20) to another section of the sand pit. Immediately out of the tunnel turn right to climb the embankment with the motorway fence on your right. Follow along this. The narrow path gradually eases away from the motorway, through a region of gorse bushes and diagonally across a rough field towards Westfields Farm and onto the farm's approach road. Here turn left for about 15 yards to find the continuing path on your right, going between fences. This brings you to a lane running from Addington to Wrotham Heath. Turn right along this road for about a quarter of a mile when you will come to a stream flowing beneath a road bridge. There is a house on the right just beyond the stream, and immediately after this, also on the right, is a footpath leading to Wrotham Heath.

This is a very pleasant stretch of path, devalued only by the sight of the motorway forcing its way through an otherwise green and verdant landscape ahead to the right. On reaching another minor road, cross straight over and keep with the path as it goes through a small patch of woodland, finally to come out at the junction of the A20 with the A25 opposite the Royal Oak pub. (Grid ref: 633580)

Wrotham Heath sits alongside the busy road. In itself it is not particularly attractive, although it has some interesting villages nearby. It boasts a Post Office Stores and public telephone kiosk almost on the Wealdway; the Royal Oak pub and a restaurant. The hotel is a Trust House Forte establishment, the Post Hotel, a short distance along the A20 north of the village street, and almost beside the motorway. Buses travel through Wrotham Heath and serve Sevenoaks and Maidstone, and various villages along the way. As the Wealdway emerges onto the main road there's a bus stop on the left which has a service to Maidstone, while that which serves Sevenoaks stands outside the Royal Oak. This is the bus stop for walkers intending to stay overnight at Kemsing Youth Hostel.

Things Seen On The Way:

1. *The Saxon Shore Way.* This long-distance walking route travels for 140 miles round the Kent coastline and finishes just over the county boundary at Rye, in Sussex. Route sheets for this walk have been published by the Kent Rights of Way Council, while there's also an

interesting book on the theme written by Alan Sillitoe and illustrated by Fay Godwin. It was published in 1983 by Hutchinson.

2. *Gravesend,* where the Wealdway begins, is a medium sized town that has lost much of its dependence upon the Thames, and with it some of its charm. In recent years it has been modernised with shopping precincts, but down where the walk begins at Town Pier by the Tilbury Ferry, there's a curious mixture of old and new. On the corner of High Street are the last few black weatherboarded buildings that give an aura of the past, while modern concrete walkways wind above the river. Not far away, in the grounds of the Parish Church of St. George, there stands an attractive statue of Pocahontas, daughter of an Indian chief, who was brought to England in the early 17th century. On her way back to the States she was brought ashore at Gravesend, and died here. In the chancel of the church, far from the wide spaces of Virginia from whence she came, she was buried in 1617.

3. *Camer Country Park,* on the B2009 between Sole Street and Meopham, consists of some 46 acres of attractive parkland, and makes a pleasant spot for a picnic. There are toilets available.

4. *London Countryway.* Another long-distance route, this circles London on a series of linking footpaths totalling 205 miles. Both Wealdway and Vanguard Way cross this. Constables publish a route guide; *The London Countryway* by Keith Chesterton.

5. *Luddesdown* has a history going back to Stone Age times; signs of dwellings of both Stone Age and Iron Age man have been found here. Roman pottery has been discovered on the slopes above this hamlet, and there are Roman tiles set in the lower walls of the church. Next door to the church stands Luddesdown Court, one of England's oldest inhabited buildings. It was once owned by Bishop Odo who came to these shores with William the Conqueror, nine hundred years ago. It has been continuously lived in since then, but unfortunately it is not open to the public.

6. *The Pilgrims Way* links Winchester with Canterbury, but it is certainly an older trackway than is suggested by its traditional use as the path of pilgrimage to the site of Becket's martyrdom. Nowadays it shares much of its route with that of the North Downs Way.

7. *North Downs Way.* Running for 141 miles between Farnham in Surrey and Dover on the Kent coast, this long-distance route sometimes traces the edge of the North Downs escarpment, sometimes runs below it. There are several route guides to it; that by Christopher John Wright and published by Constables, also includes descriptions of the Pilgrims Way and is the most readable.

8. *The Coldrum Stones,* or Coldrum Long Barrow, are owned by the National Trust and accessible at all times. What we see are the remains of a complex burial chamber raised some 2,000 years or so before Christ; massive sarsen stones, many of which have collapsed in a rough circle measuring 160 feet in circumference. Originally they would have stood upright - four of the twenty-four columns still do - with a huge covering mound of earth, and with only the entrance kept clear. This important Neolithic site forms one of a series of archaeological locations representing the 'Medway culture'. Other sites nearby are those at Addington and at Kits Coty above Aylesford on the right bank of the Medway, and they would have been joined by ancient trackways whose course is followed today by the North Downs Way.

Public Transport on Section 1:

Gravesend is served by the Tilbury Ferry from the Essex side of the Thames. The town is on a rail link with London (Charing Cross) and the Medway towns of Chatham and Gillingham. A frequent service daily. Buses by Maidstone and District; also Green Line coaches.
Sole Street lies on the London (Victoria) - Chatham railway line. M. & D. buses link with Gravesend.
Wrotham Heath has M. & D. buses to Maidstone and Sevenoaks.

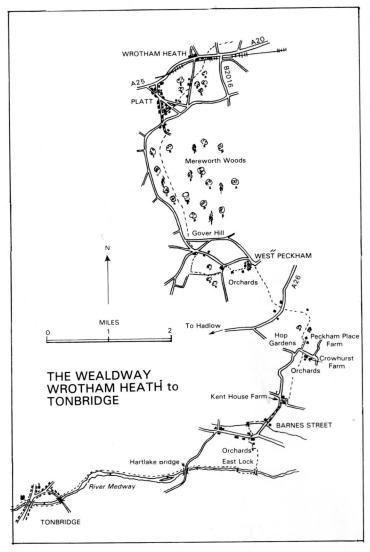

THE WEALDWAY
WROTHAM HEATH to
TONBRIDGE

SECTION 2: WROTHAM HEATH TO TONBRIDGE

Distance:	14 miles
Map:	O.S. Landranger series; Sheet 188 *Maidstone and the Weald of Kent* 1:50,000
Accommodation:	Tonbridge - Hotels, b&b
	Elsewhere - Youth Hostel in Crockham Hill (west of Tonbridge; reached by train Tonbridge -Edenbridge, then 2 miles walk).

On this section of the route there is a great variety of scenery to encounter; the hills of the greensand and low-lying meadows of the Medway. There are large tracts of woodland and orchards to wander through, short stretches of parkland, farmyards, open fields. There are some lovely villages, too, with pretty cottages and interesting old pubs, while the countryside is spotted with white-topped oast houses. This is, without doubt, the Garden of England. If you're lucky enough to catch it in blossom time, you will be captured by the sheer volume of flowering trees. The Wealdway actually wanders through the middle of several orchards; a memorable experience for the long-distance walker.

On leaving Wrotham Heath the route cuts through woods to reach the village of Platt, which has a number of splendid cottages. Then south to the expanse of Mereworth Woods with its extensive coppicing and some fine examples of ageing beeches near Gover Hill where sudden views open out to reveal the Weald in all its vast splendour. Orchards lead the walker to West Peckham, one of the prettiest villages on the 82 mile length of the Wealdway. From West Peckham the way continues into an agricultural landscape, with more large orchards and oast houses adding a touch of architectural interest. More fields, the crossing of streams that provide varied habitats for a diverse wildlife population. Out then to Barnes Street, a hamlet with picturesque buildings beside the path. Soon after this you come to Kent's major river, the Medway, and a final amble along a four mile stretch of towpath right into the heart of Tonbridge.

The Wealdway continues out of Wrotham Heath on a track that runs alongside the Fredericks Restaurant to the right of the Royal Oak pub on the A20. This track is a bridle path and it passes beneath a railway bridge after a few yards. Beyond this the way divides. Take the right fork, in effect continuing straight ahead to walk through a patch of woodland for about 500 yards until you come to a road. Turn left on the road and walk along it until you reach a drive on the right leading to a house called Wingate. The path to take leads off to the

39

right just after you pass the drive. An enclosed path with fences on either side, it is nonetheless rather attractive, especially when the rhododendrons that overhang it are in full bloom. It leads into a fine area of woodland, sloping steadily downhill. At the bottom of the slope bear left to follow the line of a fence, so to reach a white house. The path runs to the right of this, between hedges, and brings you out onto a lane. Turn right, and 30 yards farther on, go left into Potash Lane.

This route, the true line of the Wealdway, by-passes the village of Platt, going instead along its outskirts. In order to explore the village properly, or to buy provisions for the day, it is necessary to ignore the turning into Potash Lane and instead continue along the narrow road beyond for another quarter of a mile or so. You will then reach the church of St. Mary the Virgin on the right, the Blue Anchor Inn a few paces beyond, and the Post Office Stores. To return to the Wealdway, leave the church on your left and take the road forking to the right. This leads in about 500 yards to the southern end of Potash Lane at Kettle Cottage.

Potash Lane brings you past several pleasant houses to a junction with another road - that which comes from Platt, and described above - coming from the right at Kettle Cottage. Go straight ahead along the road to reach a crossroads. Cross over and continue ahead for about 200 yards. Then, where the road bends towards the left, you will find on the right the start of two bridle paths. Take the left-hand of these. There is a Wealdway marker on a tree. The track leads into Mereworth Woods.(1)

The sky had settled on the topmost boughs of the trees. It was a heavy morning, grey, cool and excessively damp. Rain came cascading through the canopy of leaves, misting the day and turning the track into dark stretches of swamp. But it brought out the fragrance of foliage, both from the trees and the wayside grasses; after a while I caught the unmistakable tang of woodsmoke. I came to a large clearing and there found a substantial tarpaulin shelter with a couple of woodmen active beneath. While rain streamed down the blackened tarpaulin, blue washes of smoke drifted out from a green-wood fire. There were no views, only the pouring rain and the mist it created, mingling with the woodsmoke, but there was a touch of enchantment about it that not even the rain could dampen. A black and white terrier came racing from the shelter; barked once out of conscience to duty, then returned to his master's side. I was left alone with the rain and the day; contented.

Farm at West Peckham on the Wealdway

There are few waymarks in the woods, but the route is fairly straightforward. It follows more or less the same direction for two miles. After an initial short stretch there are orchards on the right, then the woods close in. The track is clear, but muddy in places. There's a clearing or two then the route crosses a narrow metalled road. Shortly after this you'll see another road on the right, but the path winds above it among some fine beeches, finally to drop down to the little crossroads at Gover Hill. (Grid ref: 631529) Here are some delightful views into the Weald stretching way off to the south and the west.

Cross the road and take the bridle path which begins to the left of a white cottage, and follow it down the easy slope with broad views to enjoy as you go. At the end of the fence, turn left on a path that goes into the bottom end of the left-hand field, and follows ahead with a hedge on your right, to the field corner. There turn right onto a broad track and go left along an avenue of trees which will bring you to a road with a lodge beside a tree lined pond on your left. Another attractive vignette.

West Peckham - one of the loveliest villages on the Wealdway

Head left along the road for a few yards. Then you will see a line of white railings on the right of the road with a footpath alongside it. Take this footpath. It leads away from the road and into an orchard. The route traces the boundary of the orchard leftwards, then approaches a bungalow. On the way to it you will see the lofty landmark of Hadlow Tower(2) standing clear above the distant fields. Turn left by the bungalow, then right to go along the next orchard boundary to its end where you will find a kissing gate that brings you onto the village green at West Peckham.(3) This is an extremely attractive spot that makes a rest rather tempting. The Swan Inn, seen across the green to the right of the church, serves meals, and proudly displays a plaque to commemorate its winning an award as best country pub of the year.

Cross the green to the right of the church and go straight ahead along the village street to pass a public telephone kiosk on your right. A short distance beyond this a road leads off to the left. At this point you will find a footpath on your right. At first a broad track, it then narrows between fences. Note the pretty scene of a pond, willows and modern house set back on your left. Cross a stile and, going straight ahead, find a gate into the next field. Here turn left and follow along the edge of the field until you come to a stile with a waymark. Over this, go diagonally half-right to the corner of the field where another stile brings you into a flat meadow with a ditch running along its right-hand boundary. Follow this to the A26 Tonbridge road. (Grid ref: 653514)

Cross the road with care to the continuing footpath which begins at a gate a little to the right. The path here is not always evident on the ground. Head diagonally half left across the field towards a rather sparse line of trees marking the distant field boundary, going almost due east. By the right-hand oak tree you will find a stile. Cross this and walk through the next field with a dilapidated building about 100 yards off to your left, to reach a fence. Go over the stile and turn right to follow the fence as far as a small wood. The way leads through this, crossing a couple of little streams and along a farm track. On reaching a hop garden turn left on the track that goes towards the buildings of Peckham Place Farm. The track bears right of these and brings you onto a country road. You are now in the heart of oast house(4) country, and over the next few miles the route passes close to a number of these lovely buildings, so typical of Kent.

On the road bear left for about 100 yards to locate a stile in the hedge on the right. There is a waymark. The route now passes along the right-hand side of the large corrugated iron barns of Crowhurst Farm, whose oast houses make a fine picture. Continuing, pass some buildings on your right and head through the large orchard which, in late April and early May, should be a mass of blossom.

At the far side of the orchard cross a footbridge into a very large field. In the distance, straight ahead, you will see another cluster of oast houses. The route of the footpath makes for a point a little to the left of these, and comes out on a narrow road. Turn right and walk along the road to reach these oast houses at Kent House Farm. Just past the farm a small lane winds off to the left. Follow this for nearly half a mile, but keep alert for any traffic that may come along; drivers on quiet country roads seldom suspect that they will meet anything on what they consider to be their own private race track; walkers least of all!

On reaching Pierce Mill on your right, and a corrugated barn on the left, turn right to leave the lane, and take the sometimes faint footpath which leads along the bank of the stream; one of the sources of the Medway. The path heads among trees and along the edge of a field, and about 500 yards from the road you come to a footbridge. Cross this, then over a short stretch of field to its boundary where you turn

43

Crowhurst Farm near West Peckham

left and follow the field edge to the road at Barnes Street, to emerge facing the lovely timbered, six hundred years old Barnes Place.

Turn right along the road and just beyond the boundary of Barnes Place, turn left. You'll find yourself shortly in a farmyard with an orchard ahead. Cross a stile and head left to pass beside the farm buildings, then turn right to cross another stile leading into the orchard. Walk along the edge of the orchard beside a ditch on your left. After a while the path leads through fields until at last you come to a bridge over the River Medway.(5) (Grid ref: 647473)

It may come as something of a surprise to learn that the Medway is navigable from Tonbridge to the sea. The stretch between Tonbridge and Maidstone in particular is very popular in summer for long-boat holidays. You'll see small motor boats, too, and of course, canoeists. The four mile Wealdway section that follows as far as Tonbridge has several locks spaced along it, and should you catch craft negotiating these locks, you'll have an additional interest to brighten the day.

Cross the bridge over the Medway and turn right. At first there is no clear path, but simply follow along the side of the river until you come to East Lock a short distance away. Cross back to the northern side of the river at this first lock, then bear left and continue, now on a path, as far as the edge of Tonbridge.

Along the riverside walk there will always be much of interest, whether that be in the sighting of birds or riverbank animals, the wayside flowers or distant views. Sometimes Hadlow Tower stands proud across the fields; sometimes it is the line of the Greensand Ridge that draws the eye. Always there is something worth gazing at. It is a four mile stretch that has no parallel elsewhere along the Wealdway until you come to a short stroll in the company of the Cuckmere, deep in Sussex. The river has a character all its own and, unhurried, the walker has time to absorb the essence of it.

Almost a mile beyond East Lock the path goes under Hartlake Bridge,(6) and after this among trees before emerging into open countryside again with Tonbridge dominating the skyline. It is still distinctly rural though, until suddenly there's a hint of light industry and the path comes above the river and onto a road bridge. Cross the bridge and the road to the south side of the river, and continue along a metalled path with the Medway now on your right. This path leads to within a few yards of a most attractive bridge in the heart of Tonbridge(7) High Street, the final hundred yards or so of this stage being along a concrete walkway that forms part of a recent waterside development.

In this heart of town, Tonbridge is a pleasant, historic place of old buildings, castle ruins and gardens. As the largest town on the Wealdway after Gravesend, there should be no difficulty in finding accommodation here, nor in stocking up with supplies for the onward route. For those who intend to travel to Crockham Hill to stay overnight at the Youth Hostel there, turn left along the High Street for about 500 yards or so to find the railway station on the right-hand side of the road. Trains run westward to Edenbridge. From there you have a two mile walk north to Crockham Hill.

Things Seen On The Way:

1. *Mereworth Woods* cover an area of almost 6 square miles, with one road (B2016) running through to effectively break them into east and west. The Wealdway traverses the western section, a region mainly

devoted to coppicing with some fine mature beeches left as a screen around the viewpoint of Gover Hill. Mereworth Woods represents one of the largest areas of woodland left in Kent, and it was in these that wild boar were hunted still in the reign of Elizabeth I. Nowadays, parts of the woodland are owned by the Forestry Commission, some by the Ministry of Defence, some private and a small piece at Gover Hill, by the National Trust.

2. *Hadlow Tower.* Although not actually on the Wealdway, this lofty structure is a striking landmark from various points on this section of the walk. The tower is 170 feet high, a Gothic folly and all that remains of Hadlow Castle, a substantial house built in the last year of the 18th century. The tower was added as an afterthought by Walter Barton May, an industrialist and wealthy eccentric.

3. *West Peckham* is one of the prettiest villages of the Wealdway, and the initial view of it is a re-creation of the archetypal English village scene; a neat, well kept green on which cricket is played, some stately trees framing the centuries old church, a fine country pub and a row of attractive cottages. Around lies a green and lush countryside, and the whole setting combines to create the nostalgia that plagues ex-patriot Britons stranded in far-off lands. It was mentioned in the Domesday Book, although its church was not, despite the Saxon work in the lower portion of the tower that clearly shows its existence when the Normans arrived. Elsewhere in the church are some fine carved wooden figures behind the altar, and an interesting private pew converted from the former chantry.

4. *Oast Houses* are seen along so many sections of the walk that they deserve a word or two of explanation. These lovely conical buildings, some circular, others square edged, were originally used for the drying of hops. There would be a furnace in the lower portion, and hops stacked about and around in huge sacks, known as pockets. Whilst there are still working oasts to be found in Kent, the hop industry has changed dramatically over the years, and many oast houses have been adapted to other uses; as storage barns, for example, or turned into attractive homes. For those interested further in these buildings, a visit to the Whitbread Hop Farm at Beltring near East Peckham on the Medway, or to the Information Centre housed in an oast house at Bough Beech Reservoir, near Edenbridge, are highly recommended.

5. *River Medway.* The old distinction between Kentish Men and Men

The Medway, seen from the Wealdway

of Kent was a product of the Medway's division of the county into east and west. To the east lived Men of Kent, to the west were born Kentish Men. The river rises just beyond the county's boundary in Sussex, but by the time it has reached Tonbridge it has grown to a substantial waterway. From there as far as the sea just beyond Rochester, it is navigable. There is a splendid riverside walk that follows the Medway from Tonbridge to Maidstone; 16 miles of quiet pleasures.

6. *Hartlake Bridge*, west of East Lock on the Medway, is successor to a frail structure that was the site of a terrible accident in the autumn of 1853. It was harvest time in the neighbouring hop gardens, and as was the tradition, much of the hop picking was done by families from London's East End. After work one day two waggons loaded with hop pickers were returning to the pickers' camp when one of the leading horses broke through a bridge rail, dragging with it both waggons into the river. A total of 35 men, women and children were drowned in the accident, and Hadlow church bears a memorial to them.

47

7. *Tonbridge* had a hill fort in Iron Age times; its name is thought to derive from *'dun burgh'*, which in Old English means 'hill fort'. But it is the remains of the Norman castle, standing above the river, that distinguishes the town today. The original castle was built to defend the important river crossing not long after the Norman Conquest, but was almost completely destroyed by fire in 1087. A replacement was built immediately, which perhaps is an indication of its strategic importance.

The Wealdway wanders directly below the huge walls that remain, and alongside the motte that has been softened with gardens, shrubs and trees. Elsewhere the town contains several lovely old buildings, including the 16th century Chequers Inn not far from the castle, and another timber building of the same period next door. Up the hill a short distance away stands Tonbridge School, all mellow stone and neat lawns, founded in 1553 as a Free Grammar School. It was almost completely rebuilt in 1864 in Victorian Gothic style.

Public Transport On Section 2:

Wrotham Heath is noted at the end of Section 1.
Barnes Street has a bus link with Tonbridge run by Maidstone and District. No Sunday service at present.
Tonbridge has frequent train services to and from London (Victoria and Charing Cross) and on to various locations further south, including Ashford and Dover. A cross-country train service to Redhill and Reading goes through Edenbridge. There is also a route to Maidstone via Paddock Wood. Buses go to Barnes Street, Mereworth, Tunbridge Wells, Southborough etc. by M. & D.

*One of the many converted oast houses seen on the the Wealdway,
this is near Frodcombe*

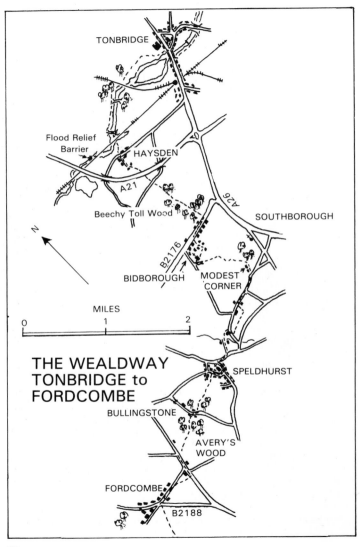

SECTION 3: TONBRIDGE TO FORDCOMBE

Distance:	9½ miles
Map:	O.S. Landranger series; Sheet 188 *Maidstone and the Weald of Kent* 1:50,000
Accommodation:	Fordcombe - b&b
	Elsewhere - Youth Hostel in Crockham Hill (north of Fordcombe and reached via Edenbridge by infrequent bus service; or alternatively by continuing on WW for 1 mile, then walk 1 mile to Ashurst Station for train to Edenbridge. 2½ mile walk Edenbridge - Crockham Hill).

In many ways this section of the route is the finest of the whole Wealdway, and one of the loveliest walks in its own right in this corner of the country. It begins with a two mile stroll along the Medway's banks, then follows with a climb through fields and woodland to the village of Bidborough, whose ridge affords an immense panorama overlooking much of the countryside walked in Section 2. From Bidborough the way continues through more delightful meadows and woods to Speldhurst, another village on a hill, then by a remote and tiny hamlet with old cottages containing an aura of the past in their timbers, and on to Fordcombe.

Throughout the day there are fine views of rolling hills and green valleys; an agricultural countryside again, but quite different from that of low lying districts of the Weald. This is the High Weald with its lush green ridges forming individual landscapes here and there, each one begging to be transformed onto an artist's canvas. Since the distance to be walked is modest, and there are few route finding difficulties to be encountered, this is a day to be taken leisurely, without an eye on the clock.

From the bridge over the Medway in Tonbridge High Street the Wealdway follows the north bank of the river. A fanciful iron gate leads into Riverside Walk and to the castle, and outside the gate there stands a board giving details of the Wealdway, together with a map of the route.

Go through the gate and follow the tarmac path that runs between the river and the castle walls, with flower beds and pleasant trees overhanging the path. The way crosses a side stream and passes a café, swimming pool and model railway on your left. Cross a narrow road and, keeping the stream on your right, continue straight ahead, along the edge of a large meadow, eventually to pass beneath a low railway bridge. After this the path crosses the side stream again, goes through

The Wealdway information board close to Tonbridge Castle

a little wooded area and turns left to cross two more side streams to gain once more the bank of the Medway proper. The route now continues on the northern bank of the river on what is known as the 'Straight Mile'.(1)

Out of Tonbridge this walk alongside the Medway is a splendid intro-duction to the day's journey; peaceful save for the birds in full song, and every now and then interesting views off to the Greensand Ridge bordering the Medway's valley to the right.

Ignore the footbridge known as Lucifer Bridge, but continue along the path that from this point is unmade, soon to stroll along the edge of meadows. Before long you come in view of the bridge that carries traffic on the A21 Tonbridge by-pass. Before it are the large grey gates of the Flood Relief Barrier. Shortly before you reach these, turn away left over a new concrete footbridge. On the south side of the river bear right to cross a couple of culverts, then left through a kissing gate and under a railway bridge.

Through another gate, go straight ahead across a footbridge, bear left immediately upon meeting another path, then bear right to cross two more footbridges. You now join a wide track straight ahead to a road at the hamlet of Haysden, with its pub, The Royal Oak, which serves snacks during opening hours. Pass to the right in front of the pub and go down the rough lane beyond. At the bottom turn left to reach a farmyard. Here bear right, pass through a gate into a field with a barn and oast house on the left, and cross the field to the far left-hand corner to find a foot tunnel under the by-pass. Through the tunnel turn left. Go over a footbridge and immediately turn right. With a hedge on your right follow along the headland of the field to reach a stile leading onto a road.

Cross the road and over a stile half-left opposite, into a field climbing to a wood crowned hill. The path goes up this field to reach a little wood, then along its right-hand edge to pass through a gateway leading to the other side. Now continue along the left-hand side of Beechy Toll Wood on a track that leads at the top of the field into the wood. Go straight ahead through this rather fine patch of woodland, still gaining height, until you emerge onto the B2176 road at Bidborough. (Grid ref: 573437) You've now reached one of the classic belvederes of this part of Kent. Turn right along the road and a few yards later you'll have a wonderful panorama out to the north.

At 475 feet above sea level you've come onto the High Weald. Looking beyond the Medway's valley deep below, the hills on the far side are those of the Greensand Ridge. Way out to the north-east is the orchard country for which Kent is famous. Beyond that are hills of the North Downs. It's all lovely country.

Continue along this road for about 500 yards, passing houses with pleasant gardens and enjoying the views for much of the way. On the left-hand side of the road, immediately before reaching the police house, you'll find a footpath with a sign pointing towards the church. Follow this path. It takes you through a small residential area, past a sports field and up a slope to enter the churchyard. There you will be greeted by another lovely sight; an ancient church perched above the rooftops of cottages, with yet another splendid panorama, this time overlooking the west.

Wander along the path through the churchyard. If the church is unlocked, spare a moment to go inside. The cool breath of ages will be a source of refreshment after the climb up the hill. From the church door go beyond and down through the lych gate onto a road. Bear left

The lovely old church at Bidborough on the Wealdway

to pass in front of the village school, and walk down Spring Lane. At the bottom, where the lane turns to the left, go straight ahead on a footpath through trees, then over a stile to reach the foot of the slope. Cross a small footbridge and head up the opposite hillside keeping a fence on your right. Find a stile beside a large oak tree. Cross this and go through the woodland to another stile leading into an open field. Bear half-right across this towards the left-hand corner of a cemetery, then follow the cemetery fence down the hillside beyond, keeping the fence on your right. In the valley bottom cross a little footbridge in front of a copse. Over this take the first path on the right, which will lead to a house. Continue along the path, with a white fence on your left. In a few moments this brings you to Modest Corner. (Grid ref: 572423)

Turn right to pass in front of a quiet row of houses, in the midst of which is The Beehive pub; as shy and secluded as you'd wish to find. Go down the slope beyond the pub, cross the cemetery access road and so reach a winding country lane. Here turn right and follow the lane as it climbs uphill for about half a mile. On the right you will see a driveway leading to several houses; the Birchetts. Opposite this, on

*The Beehive, tucked shyly among a row of cottages at Modest Corner,
near Speldhurst*

your left, there's a metal kissing gate with a footpath sign. Go through this and cross two fields, keeping a hedge on your left, to the far boundary of the second field where, instead of going through the kissing gate on your left, you must turn right and walk along the edge of the field to a stile. Continue straight ahead over two more fields with the top of Speldhurst church seen ahead among trees across a small valley. Down a slope you come to a stile and a few steps leading down onto a quiet road. (This is, in fact, the same road leading from Modest Corner.)

Turn right for a short distance, then just beyond the white house turn left and cross a stile to take the path beyond, over another stile then straight down the steep hillside to a stream at the bottom. Now go ahead on an access road to pass in front of a former mill, whose pond will be seen just beyond to the left. Continue up the lane to reach a road. Turn right and follow this to Speldhurst(2) village, taking the left fork at a road junction just before the village.

Speldhurst's position is quite delightful. It sits atop a hill with narrow roads plunging off like the legs of a spider into lovely countryside. All around lies a charming series of meadows and woodlands, with large views to entice the walker deeper into enchantment. The Wealdway leads conveniently past the George and Dragon pub, which is ideally positioned for a lunchtime halt, and is interesting in its own right. Those in need of other supplies may be able to stock up from the Post Office Stores, which is to be found some way farther along the road beyond the turn-off point for our route, indicated below.

Walk past the George and Dragon and take the right fork where the road divides by the church. About 200 yards along this road, find a kissing gate on the left with a footpath sign indicating the route to Bullingstone Lane. (Continue beyond this footpath if you wish to find the Post Office Stores.) The path leads behind some houses, then into a large open field with big views off to the right. The path comes to a stile and into a sloping woodland that brings you down into Bullingstone Lane which boasts a collection of lovely old cottages. It's a fascinating corner.

Turn right onto the lane. There's a typical Kentish tile-hung cottage standing back on the right. About forty yards along the lane go left to pass between a pair of 15th century thatched cottages set in romantic seclusion from the world. The path between them leads into Avery's Wood; another enchanting place with many fine trees, steep slopes and a footbridge over a stream. Beyond the stream the path climbs through the wood for a while, then comes to a stile. Over this head diagonally across the field making for the far left-hand corner.

Two more stiles lead out to a country road. There are ponds here on both sides of the road. Turn left and walk along it, passing after a while a converted oast house on your left. A road branches off to the right and is signposted to Fordcombe. Ignore this and continue straight ahead, passing Cleave House on your right and coming to another road junction, this time on the left. Opposite this road, on your right, a Wealdway marker indicates the route through a gate and up some steps. Passing one or two buildings, go straight ahead into a field that has a tennis court seemingly marooned in it to the left.

This field was almost completely yellow with buttercups that had grown to knee height. In the shade of a line of trees were three handsome horses, but it was not until I was almost touching them that I discovered a young foal sitting peacefully nearby - almost totally hidden by the buttercups. As he struggled to his feet the flowers reached to his belly where a yellow mark had been painted by the pollen like a plimsoll line on a ship.

A stile leads onto another road where you turn left and walk along it for half a mile, so to reach the village green of Fordcombe, and the completion of this section of the route.

Fordcombe sits at a crossroads, an attractive village with its green, its well tended playing field, its tall chimneyed houses and the Chafford Arms pub lining the B2188 Penshurst to Langton Green road. Opposite the green there's a Post Office Stores. A public telephone stands near the pub a little way down the road. There's bed and breakfast to be had locally.

Things Seen On The Way:

1. *The Straight Mile.* This stretch of the Medway west of Tonbridge represents the limits of an attempt, well over a century ago, to extend the river's navigation as far as Penshurst. The attempt petered out, but just west of the Tonbridge by-pass a basin has been formed by the damming of part of the river, and the result, Hayesden Water, is now used for sailing.

2. *Speldhurst* is a charming hill village with Saxon links, and was mentioned in a document dated AD 768. It overlooks sweeping country that lies on the edge of the Wealden iron-making region.

House with a view - Bidborough

Indeed, just outside the village to the north-west, Barden Furnace Farm occupies the site of one of the smelting works of by-gone times. The church is a sturdy Victorian replacement of an earlier Norman place of worship that was destroyed by lightning. In it there's some fine stained glass by William Morris and Burne-Jones.

Public Transport On Section 3:

Tonbridge details are noted at the end of Section 2.
Bidborough has infrequent Maidstone and District buses linking with Tunbridge Wells.
Speldhurst is also served by M. & D. buses from Tunbridge Wells.
Fordcombe has M. & D. buses linking Edenbridge, Tonbridge and Tunbridge Wells. Infrequent, and none Sundays.

Avery's Wood, Bullingstone. A magical place on the Wealdway
(between Speldhurst and Fordcombe)

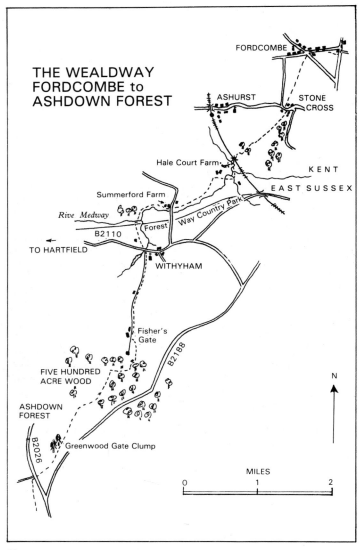

THE WEALDWAY
FORDCOMBE to
ASHDOWN FOREST

FORDCOMBE

ASHURST

STONE
CROSS

Hale Court Farm

KENT

EAST SUSSEX

Summerford Farm

Rive Medway

Forest   Way Country Park

B2110

← TO HARTFIELD

WITHYHAM

Fisher's
Gate

B2188

N

FIVE HUNDRED
ACRE WOOD

ASHDOWN
FOREST

B2026

Greenwood Gate Clump

MILES

0   1   2

SECTION 4: FORDCOMBE TO BLACKBOYS

Distance:	18½ miles
Maps:	O.S. Landranger series; Sheet 188 *Maidstone and the Weald of Kent;* Sheet 198 *Brighton and The Downs;* Sheet 199 *Eastbourne, Hastings and Surrounding Area* 1:50,000
Accommodation:	Blackboys - Youth Hostel
	Elsewhere - b&b in Buxted (2½ miles north-west of Blackboys)
	Hotel in Uckfield (4 miles west of Blackboys and 1 mile off Wealdway).

This, the longest stage of the Wealdway, is so dictated by limitations of accommodation en route. Out of Fordcombe it leads immediately into a fine countryside of rolling meadowlands that fold away to a land of streams and attractive isolated farms as Kent gives way to East Sussex. A lovely section that sets the walker fair for the day ahead.

From Withyham a long lane entices the route into a parkland-like region, steadily gaining height once more. Then into Five Hundred Acre Wood where you may be fortunate to see deer roaming. Coming out of this extensive woodland, the Wealdway then traverses the high open heath of Ashdown Forest, and crosses the path of the Vanguard Way. The route across the Forest explores its many facets, but once the way leaves this behind, the nature of the walk changes once more to one of meadow and woodland until it comes to the stately sweep of Buxted Park with its great trees and colourful rhododendrons .

The route leaves Buxted Park to drop down to the little River Uck, which it follows to Hempstead Mill before climbing over more hills with woods and meadows and attractive ponds. It then links with the Vanguard Way for a brief stretch on the outskirts of Blackboys.

On leaving Fordcombe cross the road to the playing field left of the crossroads and walk across it to the far left-hand corner where there is a stile. Over this the path continues in the same direction along the edge of two or three fields, crossing stiles now and then. There are fine views to enjoy off to the right where the fields slope down to the valley in which the young Medway meanders. Eventually the last field brings you to the right of buildings and onto the A264 East Grinstead to Tunbridge Wells road at the hamlet of Stone Cross. (Grid ref: 522390)

Note: *Those wishing to catch the train from Ashurst to Edenbridge (for*

Youth Hostel accommodation at the end of Section 3) should turn right here and follow the main road for about ¾ mile to Ashurst Station. (The line is closed on Sundays.)

Turn left and follow the road for a few yards until it curves sharply left. On the right you'll see a waymark beside a house. Go down the way indicated between fences, then out into a meadowland of great charm with woods on the left and the brow of the hill rising slightly on the right. The path, often rather faint, leads through this rolling meadow straight ahead towards an enticing view of distant hills with woodlands on their crown and chequered fields on their facing slopes. There's hardly a sign of habitation in this view; one of the finest of the whole route.

Remaining to the left of the ridge, keep ahead to cross a stile by a field gate near a cattle water trough, then towards a sloping line of trees. There are two stiles here. Take the left-hand one and follow down the slope to find a stile in the hedge on the right halfway down. Over this bear left to reach a little wood. Cross through and turn right on a faint path. (This is the Sussex Border Path.(1)) About twenty yards along this turn left into a little 'valley' towards a white gate leading under the railway.

Go through the tunnel under the railway to another white gate. Turn half-left to a footbridge over the stream that here marks the border between Kent and Sussex. Over the footbridge a waymark points across the field half-right. Aim towards a pair of oast houses seen several fields ahead. You will come to a farm track where you turn right, cross two bridges and approach Hale Court Farm, standing above the track with its single oast making a rather pleasing picture. Turn left before the farm to leave the track on a path over a stile, and go along the left-hand edge of the field. The innocent stream on the left is the Medway. The path continues in the same direction to reach a road about ¾ mile after having left Hale Court Farm.

Cross the road to take the path just to the left of Summerford Farm. Go through a gate and along the left-hand boundary of the farm, pass Dairy Cottage and take the farm track which keeps above the Medway stream and looks ahead to the spire of Hartfield church. The track enters a wood and a few yards later it is necessary to leave the track to drop down left on a rough path to the stream. Follow the stream right, then cut across the field to a footbridge leading over it. On the other side of the stream you pass over stiles bordering a dead-straight tree lined track. This is the Forest Way Country Park which takes the route of the former Forest Row to Groombridge railway line.

The Wealdway near Stone Cross - approaching Sussex

In the field beyond go straight ahead, making for a point about 50 yards left of a barn. There you will find a gate leading into the next field. Continue across this to reach a gate and a stile. Over this runs the B2110 road. (Grid ref: 493357) Turn left, cross the roadbridge over the Medway and then head right on a metalled road signposted Withyham Church.(2)

The hamlet of Withyham lies a short distance to the east along the B2110. It has a 16th century pub, the Dorset Arms, and a Post Office Stores.

Turning into the road that leads to the church, look down to the right where a lake forms a picturesque corner. The Wealdway now follows this road - it is a private road, but with right-of-way for pedestrians - for a little over a mile to Fisher's Gate. It's a glorious walk, too, that leads through a green parkland with fine stately trees and huge views, sometimes southward to Ashdown Forest, sometimes clear behind to the north over country walked earlier. Along this road are one or two attractive houses; one especially being a half timbered

*From Withyham the Wealdway goes along a scenic lane,
past this delightful thatched house and on to Five Hundred Acre Wood*

thatched building on the right, standing among a group of lofty pines. Beyond it the views are immense.

Eventually the road comes to a row of cottages and farm buildings, and ahead you'll see a gate with a notice forbidding entry. Here the path goes to the left between fences on a diversion. It then enters Five Hundred Acre Wood.(3)

The path comes to a driveway. Take the drive ahead, following it to the left of a white cottage called Forest Place. After this keep to the right-hand roadway, which after a while, drops down to a large pond on the right, seen behind a high wire fence. The roadway soon becomes a track climbing uphill. Then the woods open on the right to a field. A few yards beyond, on the left, a broad track once again enters into the woods. Go along this track for more than half a mile until you reach a fence with a gate and a stile set in it. Cross the stile where you will find one of the Wealdway marker posts that direct the route across Ashdown Forest.

These posts are unpainted oak, 2'6" high, with the route direction carved as a simple line in the top. Simple, but most effective, they are strategically placed to aid route finding throughout the Forest region, especially where crosstracks could otherwise create some confusion or doubt.

Continue through Five Hundred Acre Wood along a path aided by the waymarks for another 600 yards or so until you emerge from the cover of trees on a path that bears right at a fork and comes onto the heathland of Ashdown Forest.(4)

Almost at once you gain the impression of the Forest being a high open region of gorse and bracken, with birches growing wild and stands of Scots pine acting as landmarks. In many places you will come across the sign of summer fires, with charred bushes and blackened tree stumps; a potent reminder to smokers to be extremely cautious, especially in dry conditions. There are long views everywhere; out to the low country that moats it, out to far-off ridges of blue. The crossing of Ashdown Forest marks a considerable landmark on the journey to the sea, for from here you may be lucky enough to gain your first sighting of the South Downs, soft and watery-looking as they blend against the sky.

The path from the wood becomes a broad trail that leads steadily uphill for about half a mile to gain Greenwood Gate Clump, a lovely stand of pines that, at 720 feet, marks not only the highest part of the Forest, but quite literally the high point of the Wealdway. Continue past Greenwood Gate Clump on the trail to the left of it, still

Greenwood Gate Clump, on Ashdown Forest - The Wealdway's highest point

maintaining the same direction. Off to the left you may hear traffic on the B2188 road, but this remains unseen as yet. You come instead to another road, the B2026, opposite the drive to Old Lodge. Cross the road to the left of this drive and turn half-left along a track which later curves leftward to run parallel with the road. Walk along this track for almost a mile towards another clump of pines, Camp Hill. The Wealdway curves right to reach it.(5)

The sun was almost overpowering as I topped Camp Hill, and I was thankful for the shade thrown by the pines. Sprawling there I was entranced by the peace and apparent isolation. On a June day I was alone with the heath spread out in folding vales and gentle mouldings before me. Half an hour before I'd seen a fallow deer with her fawn. Now I listened to a symphony of birdsong. An adder was sunning itself a couple of strides away. There was the scent of pine in my nostrils, a broad view of the country I loved, and the dreamlike satisfaction that comes from moving comfortably through a landscape that has a history a thousand years old, yet remains attractive, invigorating and challenging. The Wealdway was reawakening the sense of wonder that no-one who really cares about the countryside can every truly lose.

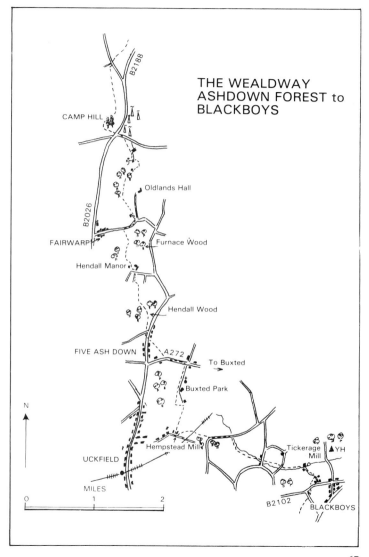

THE WEALDWAY
ASHDOWN FOREST to
BLACKBOYS

From the commemoration marker at Camp Hill bear left to reach the B2026 opposite a road junction. Cross the main road and take the minor one ahead, which is signposted to Crowborough. Very shortly the fence boundary that surrounds the lofty radio masts will be seen on your left. About 150 yards from the junction, leave the road on a path to the right, indicated by one of the wooden waymarks. Follow this path among gorse and bracken to reach a farm track and a house. Turn right and follow the track, with wide views over the south to enjoy, until it suddenly makes a right-hand bend. On the left there is stile by an oak tree. Over the stile turn right to reach another stile, and beyond this go straight ahead to a track which serves a bungalow seen to your right. Continue ahead for another thirty yards when you will find a half hidden WW waymark post signalling the path on the right. This heads down through the bracken to cross the track once more.

The path brings you to the rear of a white cottage almost submerged in a protective hollow. Go left around it, descending to meet the driveway where the path continues straight ahead across the drive and down to a small wood. Within the wood the path may be rather muddy after rain, but you soon emerge from it, cross a plank bridge and turn left past the hedge boundary of Brown's Brook Cottage. On arriving at the rough driveway that serves the house and cottages, bear left along it. The continuing path is waymarked on the right of the driveway just after you pass a gate on the left. The path climbs up to the right, crosses another driveway and makes a way amongst bracken to reach a broad bridle path going left.

Follow this track to the left for about 170 yards, when you will find the next waymark post indicating the route off to the right. The path follows beside a wood, then veers away from it to cross another broad track. Go straight across this, above a stream to the right. The path continues across the heathland to a drive. Here turn right and follow it down past a house to reach a country road and the rather grandiose iron gates of Oldlands Hall.(6) The Wealdway now leaves Ashdown Forest.

Head right along the road for about a quarter of a mile. On the left a gate leads into a sports field, and a few paces beyond this a waymark post leads off the road on a narrow path and takes you through a rough spinney.

Note: *The village of Fairwarp lies a short distance along the road beyond the Wealdway turn-off. In the village there's a pub and a Post Office Stores.*

Hendall Manor on the Wealdway

Through the spinney the path leads to a track, and a few yards along this a yellow WW arrow on a gate to the left directs the route into a field. Over this field a stile brings you into a wood with a footbridge over a stream that clearly shows traces of iron-ore in this area. Over the footbridge there's a Forestry Commission notice board announcing that this is Furnace Wood.

As its name would suggest, Furnace Wood has connections with the once important iron industry, for timber from here was used for charcoal to fire the furnaces that produced England's first cannon early in the 16th century. Note too, near the head of the wood shortly before you leave it, a rocky outcrop that looks as though it might have once been a quarry for iron-stone; now green and weathered among the trees.

Having crossed the footbridge turn right along the forest trail. It reaches a broad track, at which point go straight ahead on a narrow waymarked path that climbs very steeply among the trees, winds its way through the wood, past the rocky outcrop and shortly after emerges through a gate into a field. Cross the field towards a house

Buxted Place

seen ahead, passing to the left of it. Then go right through a gate and onto a driveway. Here turn left to pass in front of the impressive looking white fronted Hendall Manor. (Grid ref: 475257)

Go down the farm road to the right, and where it bends to the left go straight ahead over a waymarked stile and along a path bounded by hedges. This will lead to a stile and a gate, at which cross the field aiming for a point to the right of a cottage. At the right-hand end of the hedge there is another gate. Through this go straight ahead down the slope to reach Hendall Wood. The path through the wood is a delightful one. It climbs steadily, sunken for much of the way and with green moss lined banks. It comes to a stile with a field ahead. Go straight ahead over this to a fence, then through a small patch of woodland to a minor road. Across this waymarks lead through roadside bracken and clumps of gorse, and then onto the busy A26 Tunbridge Wells to Lewes road at Five Ash Down.

Cross the road to a garage, then follow down the right-hand side of the garage building. You'll come to a stile leading into fields where the route lies straight ahead with the edge of the fields to your right, then along the side of an orchard to a farm shop. (Ice creams on sale, and strawberries in season!) Continue in the same direction, passing a pond on your left, then arrive at the A272 road. Turn left and walk uphill along the road for a little over a quarter of a mile until you come to a driveway on your right near the top of the hill by a telephone kiosk. This marks the entrance to Buxted Park.

Note: *Buxted village lies a further ¾ mile along the main road beyond the Park entrance. In the village there are shops, Post Office, pubs and b&b accommodation. There is also a railway station on the Uckfield-Edenbridge Town-East Croydon-London line. (No services on Sundays.)*

Turn right into Buxted Park(7) from the A272 and wander along the driveway until you pass Buxted Place. Continue ahead beyond the drive and take the path which goes down the slope. Halfway down this turn left on a crossing path towards a cottage. The path runs along the right-hand side of the cottage towards a stream seen ahead. Just before the stream turn sharp right and walk along the right bank of it for about 300 yards. Cross over a bridge and go through a kissing gate, then continue beside the stream. The path leads beside some cottages and brings you to a quiet lane with Hempstead Mill on your left.

Note: *For a diversion to Uckfield, with its shops, Post Office, pubs, hotel accommodation and rail link with East Croydon and London (not on Sundays), turn right on this lane (Hempstead Lane) and follow along it for a little over a mile.*

On the lane turn left, cross the stream (River Uck) and then immediately go left again over a stile onto a brief stretch of path that runs between fences and comes to another stile leading into a field. Across the field, standing at the head of the opposite slope, you will see some buildings. The path, unclear on the ground, heads across the field aiming to the left of the buildings, to find a footbridge over another stream. Beyond this the path heads up the slope to cross other stiles, bearing left of a silo. Continue ahead until you see a piece of white painted fencing with a stile. This allows access down to a crossing of the railway in a deep cutting. Over the railway climb the steps on the far side to a large field that stretches beyond. The way lies half-left across this and into a spinney. Turn right through the trees so to come out at a bend in a country road opposite the rather attractive setting of Highlands Pond.

Delaying for a while I watched dragonflies winging their way to and fro

Highlands Pond on the Wealdway approach to Blackboys

over the pond. It was a quiet place without anglers, with no traffic on the road, and only the busy hum of early summer in the air. Now and then a fish came up for an incautious insect, leaving a swelling circle of ripples as the only indication of movement. But as I set off again my eye was attracted into the field to the left of the road, and there, a hundred yards away, stepped four deer. They were almost head high amongst the green wheat, but quite unconcerned that I should be watching their trespass. My day's tally of wildlife was growing.

Turn left along the road for a little under half a mile. The road crosses a stream, but immediately before the bridge, take the stile on the right and the path which continues from it along the river bank. The route continues to follow the stream, crosses two or three stiles then crosses a footbridge. Turn right to reach a narrow road opposite a farm. (Grid ref: 505212)

Go straight ahead, walk through the farmyard, then bear right towards the stream, which you now follow round the edge of fields to another narrow road. Cross this and go half-left in the field to reach a gate, and on to eventually reach the attractive Tickerage Mill with its pond and rather fine house. Here the Wealdway combines for a brief stretch with the Vanguard Way.

Turn right to pass between the mill and the house onto the access drive. Head up the drive to reach a gate across the drive, and through this onto a metalled road. The path continues by turning right beside a house named Pippins. It then crosses a field, over a stile and reaches another which leads directly onto the B2102 road a little west of the village of Blackboys. (Grid ref: 516205)

Note: *For those planning to stay overnight at Blackboys Youth Hostel, turn left and walk along the road for about ⅓ mile, then go left along Gun Road. The hostel will be found half a mile along this on the right.*

Blackboys Youth Hostel: *A set of wooden hutments, originally built to house Spanish Civil War refugees, standing in pleasant woodlands. Simple grade, it has beds for 40 in dormitories. Hot showers, self-catering facilities, small store. No meals provided. Camping permissible in the grounds. See the current YHA Guide for up to date information on opening dates and times, and also for present charges. Telephone: Framfield (082582) 607.*

Blackboys is a small village whose name is supposedly derived from the charcoal burners of a previous age; ie: 'blackboys'. Much of the village is fairly modern, but the Blackboys Inn was built as a farmhouse in 1389, and converted as an Inn early in the 18th century. All around lies a landscape of farmland and woods, with a hint of the Downs far off in the south.

Things Seen On The Way:

1. *Sussex Border Path.* A series of paths linked together in a circuit of the county, totalling about 200 miles. The usual start is at Emsworth, on the Hampshire border, and travels clockwise to Rye.

2. *Withyham Church* stands on a hill with a lovely view; a 14th century construction that was extensively rebuilt in 1672 following severe damage by lightning. The Sackville Chapel is the pride of the church; there are numerous monuments to the Sackville family, and their family vault contains fifteen generations. Among the many memorials here is an unpretentious tablet dedicated to the writer, Victoria Sackville-West, who died in 1962.

3. *Five Hundred Acre Wood* is an extensive mixed woodland of beech, oak and conifers on the edge of Ashdown Forest, of which it once

formed part. It was enclosed in 1693 in order to be re-afforested, and in 1970 the owner of the wood dedicated the path through as a right-of-way in recognition of European Conservation Year. The wood is known to have been one of the settings for the 'Pooh' stories of A.A.Milne, who lived in nearby Hartfield.

4. *Ashdown Forest.* This roughly mid-way point along the Wealdway is all that remains of the huge Forest of Anderida, known to the Romans. During Saxon times a great deal of clearing took place, so that while all the surrounding area was settled by the time the Normans arrived, the high ground of today's Ashdown Forest was the only part without any real settlements. Today the Forest consists of more than 6,000 acres of open heathland; over the centuries the tree cover - real forest - was taken for ship building purposes, for the construction of homes, for fuel to power the iron industry, and for firewood. During the Middle Ages most of the Forest was claimed as hunting ground and divided between the more powerful landowners, leaving Commoners to fight for the right to graze their pigs and collect firewood. It was a 700 year struggle. Today, Ashdown Forest is controlled by the Board of Conservators, a group established in 1885 for the express purpose of exercising jurisdiction over all matters concerning the Forest.

5. *Camp Hill.* Standing at 650 feet above sea level on Ashdown Forest, Camp Hill grants superb views over the Forest and out to the South Downs. It was here, in a ceremony in September 1981, that the Wealdway was officially opened. There is a waymark post bearing a commemorative plaque to this effect beside the clump of pines that mark the hilltop.

6. *Oldlands Hall* stands some way back along a private drive; the Wealdway passes its great iron gates. Five hundred years ago the estate, with its ponds and dams, was heavily involved in the Wealden iron industry. What is today a peaceful countryside would once have resounded to the clanging of massive hammers. There would have been the creaking of water-wheels, the hiss and steam of red-hot metal, the roar of the furnace. In a nearby field considerable deposits of ash were found of an age to indicate that the Romans were smelting here, too. Remains of a Roman building have been found, and numerous pieces of pottery dating from the first century AD, and even skeletons. Innocent though it appears to the passer-by, this is a corner deep in a colourful history.

7. *Buxted Park* is a rolling grassland with stately trees and large shrubs. At its entrance stands Hogg House, built by Ralph Hogg the iron founder who made England's first cannon in the 16th century. Farther along the driveway is the church of St. Margaret the Queen, built in 1250 and containing a chest some 700 years old. It was first built to serve no less than seven present day parishes. A little beyond the church is the white painted mansion of Buxted Place, set behind the ornate statuary of its entrance.

Public Transport On Section 4:

Fordcombe details are given at the end of Section 3.

Withyham is on the Maidstone and District Tunbridge Wells to East Grinstead bus route.

Uckfield has Southdown bus services to Tunbridge Wells, Lewes and Brighton. Also rail link with East Croydon and London. (Not Sundays.)

Buxted is served by S.D. buses, though infrequent. Also on the Uckfield, East Croydon, London railway line.

Blackboys is served by S.D. buses on the Uckfield to Eastbourne route. Also, rarely, to Brighton and Canterbury.

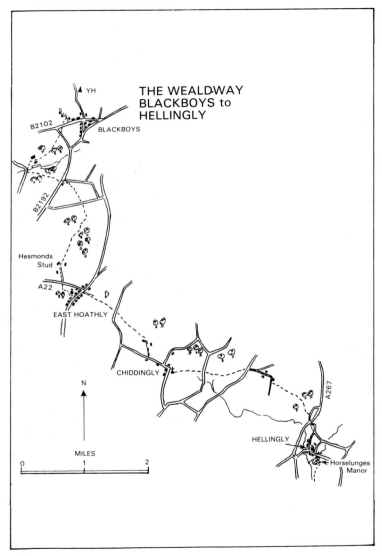

THE WEALDWAY
BLACKBOYS to
HELLINGLY

SECTION 5: BLACKBOYS TO WILMINGTON

Distance:	17½ miles
Map:	O.S. Landranger series; Sheet 199 *Eastbourne, Hastings and Surrounding Area* 1:50,000
Accommodation:	Wilmington - Hotel
	Elsewhere - b&b in Upper Dicker (north of Wilmington - on route) hotels, b&b and Youth Hostel in Alfriston (2½ miles south-west of Wilmington)

The Wealdway eases itself into a region of low country south of Blackboys. Gone are the wooded ridges of the High Weald and their broad panoramas. Behind now are the open heaths of Ashdown Forest. But once again the route explores a rich farmland with little woods and some pleasant small villages. East Hoathly, five miles from Blackboys, gives the opportunity to re-stock with provisions, then comes a stretch of mixed arable and pasture-land before coming to Chiddingly where the Wealdway crosses the Vanguard Way once more.

Again, farmland. Varied and interesting on the way to Hellingly, a little village with a lovely church set in an almost circular churchyard lined with pretty cottages. This is the beginning of the Cuckmere Valley, so far as our route is concerned, but a little way south of Hellingly a new housing development has meant a slight re-routing through Upper Horsebridge before dropping back to the river near historic Michelham Priory, a short distance from Upper Dicker. There follows a delightful section through meadows with the Cuckmere winding under willows and the Downs growing larger ahead. The hamlet of Arlington is briefly touched before the way crosses the strangely flat farmland on the final stride to Wilmington and the start of the glorious downland section that leads inevitably to the sea.

Continuing the Wealdway route from its arrival on the B2102 just west of Blackboys village, cross the road, turn right and walk along the road for about 100 yards until you come to a waymarked stile on the left. The path beyond keeps to the right-hand edge of the field and leads to another stile by a white cottage, and onto a country lane. Here turn left and, 50 yards later, you will find a stile on the right by a gate. Cross into the field and go along the left-hand side of it, then in the same manner through the next field to reach a large wood. A gate leads into the wood and the route becomes a broad and sometimes muddy track.

Coming across the fields in the cool of morning I was struck by the apparent stillness and lack of hedgerow activity. A few jackdaws were spiralling above the wood ahead, but as I drew closer, so it became apparent that every bird for miles around had gathered there for a breakfast-time woodland concert. From the peace of the fields I was transported into a concert hall of foliage, and the muddy track became for me the auditorium. I walked slowly through, enjoying to the full the very personal concert arranged for my sole benefit. Then, as I emerged from the woods, I came face to face with a South American llama; a refugee from the Andes. Nothing could have been more incongruous than this meeting; a bizarre moment that shook me instantly from the reverie inspired by the very Englishness of the songs from the trees.

The track leaves the woods and comes to the buildings of Newplace Farm, site of a former iron foundry. It's a magnificent place. On the left there is an impressive mansion, on the right the farm buildings. The driveway turns left alongside landscaped gardens with their little waterfalls running idyllically from a lake among trees and shrubs and trim lawns. The Wealdway fortuitously gives a glimpse of this magical place and sets the day on bright foundations.

At the bottom of the drive you pass through the gateway and onto a lane. Turn left. A few yards later the lane bends to the right, but straight ahead you will see a stile with a waymark indicating the continued route alongside the wood, now on your left beyond a fence. Go straight ahead on the edge of the field until the wood ends, then continue through the field aiming for the left-hand edge of a wood on the far side of the field. There is almost a line of woodland with a gap dividing it in two. The portion of wood to aim for is that to the right of the gap. Go through the broad gap where you will find waymarks leading through a gate and into the next field. Go straight across this to find a stile in the hedge about 100 yards to the right of a house which can be seen standing beside a road. (Grid ref: 517191)

This field was June-deep in lush grass, soon to be cut for hay. As I wandered through it I came upon a series of flattened 'nests' where animals had been sleeping overnight. They were too small to have been made by cattle and there were no sheep to be seen. I wandered on then, quietly keeping my eyes open and wondering what had been using this meadowland for a night's rest. Suddenly I found the answer; eighteen deer, head and shoulders only, blinking in the morning. They kept their distance. I kept mine. I would not disturb them. Though they had strayed from the line of the path, I would keep their trespass secret. We parted company with no more than a wink of acknowledgement.

Turn left on the B2192 road. About 100 yards along this a minor road, signposted Waldron, breaks away to the right. Go down this for 100 yards to find a stile by a bungalow on the right. Over this bear half-right to reach another stile, then again half-right over the field and down the slope on the far side. At the foot of the slope near a tele-graph pole go into the scrub filled hollow where a little stream snakes through. There you will find a half hidden waymarked stile. Up the other side another stile leads into the next field. Now bear half-right once more and cross this field to reach a stile in the far hedgerow near some overhead power cables. Beyond the stile is a lane. Cross this to find the continuing path. This runs parallel with the right-hand edge of a field and leads down to another tree choked hollow. The path enters this about fifteen yards left of the field corner. Go over a footbridge and emerge into the next field. Cross to the lone oak tree standing in the middle of this, and on reaching it turn sharp right over the field. You will then reach a couple of stiles and a plank bridge. In the field beyond bear half-left, pass between some massive pylons and make for the wood seen ahead.

A waymarked stile indicates the way into Great Wood, which is not so great since it has been subjected to much clearance in recent years. The path leads through and emerges to wide views. Coming out of the wood go straight ahead to cross a stile and a plank bridge, then continue ahead on a grassy track with a wooden fence on your right. The South Downs are seen ahead across a green countryside of meadows and trees. A farm comes into view. Then the track leads onto a concrete road. In the fields there are often to be seen some magnificent horses with their foals, for the farm ahead is, in fact, Hesmonds Stud. The route goes past a courtyard of stables, while the mansion called Old Whyly stands off to the left behind a screen of rhododendrons. On to the drive which becomes a tree lined avenue, and at its end you come onto the summer madness of the A22 Eastbourne road just west of the village of East Hoathly. The continuing path leads directly into the village.

Cross the road with caution. On the other side you will find a stile by a gate. Cross this and go round the left-hand edge of the field to another stile, found on your left. Go over this and follow along the right-hand edge of this field beside a wood. The path brings you to the village school of East Hoathly,(1) and out by the lovely church. Go through the churchyard and out by the lych gate. Straight ahead now over Rectory Close to the main road. Here turn left, cross the road and take the first turning on the right, which is Buttsfield Lane.

Note: *For those requiring refreshments or provisions, continue along the main road beyond Buttsfield Lane for 50 yards into the heart of the village, there to find a pub offering bar snacks and meals; also village shops and Post Office.*

Go down Buttsfield Lane, and where the road forks, bear left. So reach a stile and beyond into fields with the route continuing along a clear path. More stiles. The path goes through the edge of a little wood. Out of this continue straight ahead with a hedge on the left, and come onto a country lane.

For the next mile and a half the Wealdway runs parallel with the Vanguard Way, the latter being ¾ mile to the north. The two routes cross in the next little village; Chiddingly.

Over the lane a gate directly opposite grants access to the next field section. Continue straight ahead over a series of fields. In many instances there is no obvious path to be seen, but waymarks are to be found at strategic points. There are no real problems. Please remember to close gates behind you where the route leads through. At last you come to a farm road at Frith's Farm. (Grid ref: 538149) Follow this road until it brings you onto a motor road. Turn left and walk along this for a little under half a mile to reach Chiddingly.

As you walk along this road, note the curious Place Farm on the right; a mass of bricks built around parts of the Tudor Chiddingly Place. The original was built by the grandson of one of the more important of the first Queen Elizabeth's officials, Sir John Jefferay, whose monument stands in the village church ahead.
In Chiddingly there is the Six Bells pub (closed on Mondays), a Post Office Stores and a delightful church. Spare a few moments from the walk to go inside the church. It's an interesting, lovely building. It offers welcome cool on a hot summer's day, but more than that, it can bring a sense of tranquility and the calm of ages to add a boost to the day's journey.

Walk along the approach road to the church, keeping it on your right. Just beyond the churchyard entrance a stile on the left takes you into a field. Bear half-right to cross this. There are mid field stiles where wire fences run, and the route goes over these and down the slope beyond to a wood. Waymarks lead over a stream, then straight

Tile-hung cottages that line Hellingly churchyard

ahead up the slope beyond through the wood. Once out of the trees
cross the field to its far left corner and by way of a stile onto a quiet
country road. (Grid ref: 553143)

Turn left on this road for 25 yards where you will see a stile on the
right. Over this keep the hedge on your left, cross two more fields to a
footbridge leading over a stream, and on to a copse. Go through the
copse, then straight ahead over the field beyond to a stile at a bend in
the hedge on the far side. There is a stile with a waymark. Cross this
and head diagonally over the next field to a stile leading onto a road
near a farm with an oast house. This is Gatehouse Farm, an attractive
spot with its pond beside the road. Turn left on the road, then right at
a road junction towards Coggers Cross. About 300 yards along this
road, where it curves away to the left, a farm road leads off to the
right, going to West Street Farm and Rock Harbour Farm. Walk
along this until you come to West Street Farm standing on the left
beside a pond. Here turn right to pass Rock Harbour Farm. There is a
barn at the entrance to the farm, and immediately past this on the left
you'll find a gate and a stile. Over this and the next two stiles go
straight ahead. Come to a gate, then more stiles by some trees.

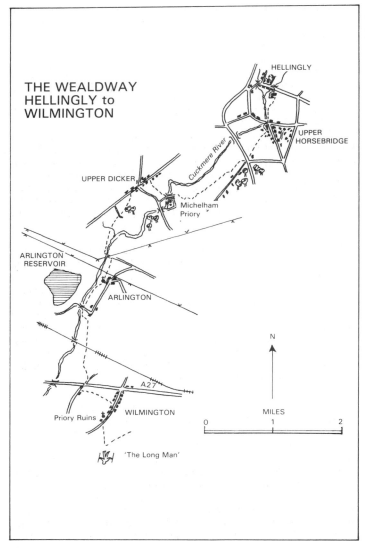

THE WEALDWAY
HELLINGLY to
WILMINGTON

HELLINGLY

UPPER
HORSEBRIDGE

Cuckmere River

UPPER DICKER

Michelham
Priory

ARLINGTON
RESERVOIR

ARLINGTON

N

A27

MILES

WILMINGTON

Priory Ruins

0   1   2

'The Long Man'

Crossing now to the left, go over one further stile with the edge of this field on your right. You reach a wood on the right with a stile in the hedge beside it. Cross over and go down the slope to the left as far as a footbridge. Over this and up the other side, then across a field to another footbridge. The way continues towards a house called Lealands. On reaching a fence cross the stile and follow round to the right of the house. Cross a track and head half-right over the next fence and through trees onto a narrow road down some steps. Turn right to reach the busy A267 road. (Grid ref: 581131)

Cross the road and head right for a few yards as far as a minor road branching off left. Turn along this to find some steps on the right a few yards later. At the top of the steps you'll come to a stile. On the path go half-left up the field to a gate giving onto a road. Turn right along this, and right again where it forks. This leads shortly to the lovely hidden village of Hellingly.(2) On reaching the church, enter the churchyard and go left on a path beside a row of neat cottages, and out at the south gate - the second gateway you meet on entering the churchyard.

When I passed through it was midday and the sun was burning. I sought the shade of one of the large trees to the east of the church and sprawled in the long grass at its base to rest and to eat my lunch. Midday and the grass was seething with insect activity. Part of the churchyard had recently been mown and the warm air was eye wateringly rich with the scent of hay. A softly spoken lady tended a grave not far away from where I rested, and passed a few moments of small-talk conversation with me before she went home to her own lunch, carrying with her the brown curled remains of last week's flowers. I was left alone with the spiders, ants and grasshoppers; with the butterflies and beetles and all the company of departed souls that once walked Hellingly's meadows and now lay quietly by.

Leaving Hellingly churchyard by its south gate, take the road ahead for a short distance until you come to the Cuckmere river. Over this, half hidden in the hedge on the right there is a kissing gate. The path beyond this leads half-left across the field to another kissing gate. Through this you have the moat of Horselunges Manor on your right; a most attractive scene. Ahead you reach the drive to the manor. Cross it and go slightly left between outbuildings and garages to find yet another kissing gate into a field. Bear right and follow along the right-hand edge of this field with the stream flowing hidden off to the right. The route soon comes to the lofty building of Horsebridge Mill. Turn left at the mill, pass beneath an archway and come out on the A271.

The route from here has been diverted from its original line because of a new housing development. At the time of writing, building work was in progress, but I am assured that the following description is the officially adopted new line of the Wealdway.

Turn right, cross the road and walk along it for about 100 yards. Now head left on a road leading to some houses. Take the first turning on the left up the rise, then after the third house on the right go along a footpath between this and the next house. This will come to a field gate. Continue ahead with houses on your left. The path veers to the right to pass over a culvert and through a metal gate. Ahead, across a large field, you will see some farm buildings. Make for the right-hand side of these. Cross a stile and go straight ahead to another stile leading out to the A22 Eastbourne road. (Grid ref: 576104)

With due care and attention cross the road and bear left for twenty yards to find a stile taking you onto a path which leads straight ahead along the edge of a field. On coming to a stile and a field gate cross over and turn left. Now keep in the same direction for a little over a quarter of a mile. Hempstead Farm is seen off to the left. The route continues ahead with Wealdway markers in strategic positions - which is just as well since the paths are often either faint on the ground or swallowed by growing crops.

With Hempstead Farm now behind you the route keeps to the edge of several fields, bearing right towards a pond, then away again over a stile, always keeping to the headland of fields. Signposts direct you until you come to a narrow field and a slope that leads down to a stream. Cross this over a footbridge and a stile. Ahead now stretches a large field. Head across this slightly right in a S.S.W. direction. On the far side of this field there are woodlands with a hedge running between them. You will find a stile with a waymark in a corner of the field between woods. Over this stile go diagonally half-left across a smaller field to a hedge with a gate in it. Through this you come to another stile and a gate on the right. The Cuckmere will be seen on the left, and across it is Michelham Priory,(3) moated with the river's aid.

Cross the Cuckmere by way of a brick bridge, and follow along the track to cross a second bridge; this time over the moat. Continue for a few yards until you see a signposted stile on the right. Over this go diagonally up the field to the opposite hedge where a double stile will be found. Go half-right across the next field towards a row of buildings. The path leads beside a fence then between two buildings, one of which is the village stores. This is Upper Dicker.

Continue ahead to reach the B2108 road where you now turn left.

Follow the road for about a quarter of a mile. On the right you will see the Plough Inn, and shortly after you have passed this, a stile with a waymark on the left takes the route away from the road and into fields once more. Half-right ahead you come to a second stile. Over this cross a field with a hedge on your right. This brings you to yet another stile where the continuing path goes ahead with a wood on your left. There are some lovely views of the Downs rolling as a blue tinted barrier to the south. The path comes to a farm road by a pond and a cottage. Turn left and a few yards later take the stile on the right to cross a field to a gate. Now head a little left down to another stile beyond which you come to a footbridge over a stream. Ahead of you stretches a large field with the Cuckmere River flowing along its left-hand boundary. The definitive Wealdway route goes straight ahead across this field, but to have the river for company is really a better proposition. By wandering along its right bank there is the chance of seeing more wildlife, and you will still reach the same crossing point as that of the official line.

The river was refreshingly clear. It was tranquil, indolent almost, and its calm induced a slackening of pace. There was no point in hurrying. Birds were singing among the bankside trees and there were dragonflies darting to and fro. I eased off the rucksack and lay contentedly beside a weir and let the day soak in. It's a lovely river, is the Cuckmere, rising as it does among hills of the High Weald it works its way quietly and without fuss through meadows and around a handful of villages before coming to the South Downs. There it has eased a channel through the chalk to find the sea at Cuckmere Haven (so enchantingly explored on the Vanguard Way). Of the four rivers that have breached the Downs, the Cuckmere is the smallest and the shortest, but its charm is obvious and no less for the modesty of its size. It's a walker's river; a delightful companion that makes no demands. It does not intrude with the boisterous non-stop chattering of a mountain stream, rather it inspires a dream-like quality into a warm summer's afternoon. I dreamed on its banks and was thankful.

The cross-field path and the river bank route both come to a gate. There's also a footbridge and a stile that lead onto a farm track. Go left along this and over Sessingham Bridge - a grand name for an unremarkable river crossing - which marks the southern boundary of what was Michelham Priory deer park. Across the bridge a few yards on the right you will find a stile in the hedge. Over this head up the slope of the hill, to pass beneath power lines, aiming to the right of a barn. Here there is another stile with the continuing path going along the left-hand edge of the next field. Waymarks lead you over stiles and a plank footbridge, through a little copse and into Arlington churchyard.(4)

Cross through the churchyard to reach a roadway. If you turn left, in a 100 yards you'll come to the Yew Tree Inn (which serves snacks) and a public telephone kiosk. But the Wealdway route lies to the right, where you come to a stile with a waymark. Go half-left across the field, through the gate and ahead to a stile in a sturdy wooden fence. Arlington Reservoir is seen off to the right, the Downs drawing closer ahead. The route now bears left, crosses a footbridge and a stile, then directly ahead over large tussocks of grass and reeds. Along the right-hand fence of a farm a stile leads onto a road which serves the water authority houses on your left. Go along this roadway, cross a stile by a gate, and cross the public road ahead. (Grid ref: 537068)

Take the path opposite with the Cuckmere again flowing beside you to the right. After a short distance the path breaks away from the river, turns sharp left and follows along the field boundary with a hedge and ditch on your right, to reach a double stile. Over these turn right and climb the slope ahead, still with a hedge on your right. At the top of the slope drop down to cross a ditch and go through a gate to reach a farm track. Cross the railway line and bear half-left over a rough field. Cross two stiles and keep a ditch on your left. After a while cross the ditch and continue in the same direction. This will bring you to a broad track that in turn leads to the A27 Lewes to Polegate road. There is a bus shelter nearby.

Cross the main road and go down the quiet country road opposite. This leads to the hamlet of Milton Street and, to Alfriston about two miles away, for those intending to spend the night there. About 150 yards along this minor road the Wealdway continues on a footpath leading left, signposted to Wilmington. It is a clearly defined path which takes you by way of a series of stiles over fields and by a nursery for about half a mile, and brings you into the main street of Wilmington.

Of all the attractive villages in Sussex, Wilmington has one of the loveliest streets. Lined with delightful cottages and overhung with fine trees, it has the presence of the South Downs rising in a green and majestic wall behind. It's an old village, going back to Saxon times, while the figure of the Long Man, cut in chalk on the Downs at the end of the street, may well date from the Bronze Age. There's also a lovely flint walled church with a 12th century chancel, and next door the remains of a Norman priory founded before 1100. In the churchyard there stands an ancient yew tree, supported

The Medway in Tonbridge

by props and chains, that may even have been standing when the church was built.

For hotel accommodation in Wilmington, bear left along the village street as far as the junction with the A27.

Things Seen On The Way:

1. *East Hoathly* is a pleasant village unfortunately sliced by a very busy road. The mediaeval church, right on the Wealdway, has a 15th century tower, while the remainder was largely rebuilt in 1856. The doorway, dating from Tudor times, is decorated with a symbol representing the Pelham Buckle. The buckle is a sword buckle said to have been presented by King John II of France to a member of the Pelham family - a local landowning family - after the battle of Poitiers in 1356.

2. *Hellingly* is a very small village consisting of a few houses, some splendid tile-hung cottages, a superb late 14th century timber built manor nearby with an idyllic moat around it (Horselunges Manor), and a quite lovely church. The circular churchyard is a unique feature, set upon a mound to follow the tradition of pre-historic burial grounds. It has its first mention in a document of 1121.

Footpath on the South Downs

3. *Michelham Priory.* This has a fascinating history. The Priory was founded in 1229, but following the Black Death a hundred years later, it went into decline. Under Henry VIII came the Dissolution of the Monasteries, and much of the original priory buildings were dismantled and the refectory turned into a farmhouse. In 1559 the main Tudor wing was built by Henry Pelham (see details above concerning the Pelham family under East Hoathly heading). Today Michelham Priory is in the hands of the Sussex Archaeological Trust who administer it with loving care. There is much for the visitor to see, besides the main building, including a 14th century gatehouse with hearths exhibiting fine Sussex ironwork and walls adorned with brass rubbings from a number of the county's churches. Nearby stands a dove-cote, built about 1800. There is also a substantial Tudor barn with a varied collection of paintings and in the yards there are old waggons. In addition there's a blacksmith's museum, wide lawns and a lovely moat. A restored watermill produces flour for sale to visitors. Michelham Priory is a fascinating place that is well worth making a return visit properly to explore.

4. *Arlington* is a hamlet with some attractive features and a long history. The church is certainly very old for it contains Saxon features, and beneath the chancel there is the base of a Roman archway which suggests that a previous building was used as the foundation for the present church. Whether this was a Roman temple we may not know,

88

Wilmington the village street that leads to the South Downs

but there are Roman bricks incorporated into the fabric of the building. Nearby, to the south of the church, there is evidence of a former settlement, much larger than present day Arlington.

Between the hamlet and Berwick Station lies Arlington Reservoir which was constructed in 1971; a good site for bird watching.

Public Transport On Section 5:

Blackboys details are given at the end of Section 4.

East Hoathly is on the Southdown bus route which runs between Eastbourne and Heathfield.

Hellingly shares the same bus service as East Hoathly.

Horsebridge has S.D. buses as with East Hoathly and Hellingly. In addition, East Grinstead to Eastbourne S.D. service on weekdays, and also weekday service between Hailsham and Uckfield via Horsebridge.

Wilmington has Southdown buses to Eastbourne, Alfriston and Seaford.

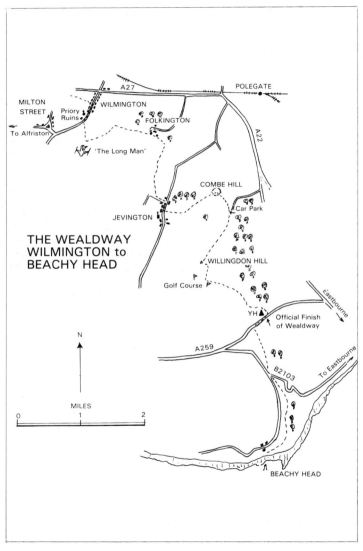

MILTON STREET

WILMINGTON

FOLKINGTON

Priory Ruins

To Alfriston

A27

POLEGATE

A22

'The Long Man'

COMBE HILL

Car Park

JEVINGTON

THE WEALDWAY
WILMINGTON to
BEACHY HEAD

WILLINGDON HILL

Golf Course

Eastbourne

YH

Official Finish
of Wealdway

A259

To Eastbourne

B2103

N

MILES

0   1   2

BEACHY HEAD

SECTION 6: WILMINGTON TO BEACHY HEAD

Distance:	9 miles
Map:	O.S. Landranger series: Sheet 199 *Eastbourne, Hastings and Surrounding Area* 1:50,000
Accommodation:	Eastbourne - Youth Hostel (Beachy Head), Hotels and b&b

This final stage of the Wealdway is a constant delight. It climbs onto the South Downs outside Wilmington village to the very feet of the huge chalk figure of the 'Long Man', then traverses the hillside with wonderful views stretching far off across the flat country in the north-west. It is a splendid pathway that trades open views for a woodland stretch that descends to Folkington church. Then up again on a long track to cross through a saddle in the Downs branching south to enter a tight vale with the village of Jevington squeezed in its restricting slopes.

From Jevington once more the path climbs into the sky, up to Combe Hill where our Neolithic ancestors made a 'causewayed camp' and later, in the Bronze Age, men came to bury their dead. Up there wheatears dart about; in spring and early summer the grass turns speckled yellow with cowslips. There are orchids on the Downs and skylarks hanging overhead. And views that seem to encompass all the earth.

From Combe Hill the Wealdway traces a ridge to Willingdon Hill with the sea sparkling off to the left and the folding Downs all green and smooth in gentle mouldings to the right. Over Willingdon Hill the route starts to descend towards the outskirts of Eastbourne, then veers away to climb the coastal Downs up to the spectacular look-out point of Beachy Head and journey's end - a world away from the Thames-side of Gravesend.

From the point where the Wealdway entered Wilmington's street, turn right and walk through the village to reach the church and Priory ruins at the head of the rise. There you have a magnificent view of the Downs ahead and the 'Long Man of Wilmington'(1) standing before you. Continue along the road for a further 250 yards, then take the bridle path on the left which rises between fences towards the feet of the chalk figure.

There are many theories as to the origin of the Long Man, and there is a plaque below the figure which outlines them. Whatever its original meaning, and whoever created it, for the Wealdway wanderer it forms an intriguing feature of the route.

*England's largest chalk figure - 'The Long Man of Wilmington'
on the Wealdway*

The path heads off to the left by the explanatory plaque, and gradually rises along the slope of the Downs with enormous views opening before you. This is one of the finest stretches of path throughout the Wealdway; a clear path, it comes to the northern end of a spur, goes through a gate and heads south-eastwards in the shade of some lovely trees, steadily leading downhill to Folkington.

It was along this downland path, open to the sun and with the huge panorama before me, that I overtook the only other walker I had met since setting out from Gravesend. An elderly gentleman with a sun-and-wind brown face, and with snow white hair puffing from under his cap, he told me that he had walked that day from Lewes and was on his way to Polegate, not far off. This, he told me, was a regular stroll; the highlight of his week. He had been retired for ten years and had walked this path almost every week since then. It was not, he assured me, a stroll he could ever tire of. I believed him.

Downland path between Wilmington and Folkington

The path rises to the right of Folkington's lovely old flint and stone church set among trees. Soon the trail becomes a sunken path between bushes and trees, climbing steadily towards converging hills. Between the hills there dips a saddle and the path makes for this. There is no possibility of losing the path for it is enclosed by hedges and trees for most of the way, unfortunately screening the best of the views. After reaching the saddle, unseen, the route now begins to slope downhill. On being joined by a track from the right, bear left, so coming to the road at Jevington.(2) (Grid ref: 654019)

Turn right and walk along Jevington's street as far as the Eight Bells pub. Almost opposite this on the left-hand side of the road, a waymark indicates the continuing route. This leads up several steps to a path which climbs a long slope once more onto the Downs. Crossing a stile bear left, gaining height steadily. Halfway up the slope there are two stiles in a fence. Cross the left-hand of these and continue straight ahead towards the crest of the hill. You come to the summit of Combe Hill(3) (630 feet above sea level) with its glorious views.

Combe Hill is one of the very finest of all the vantage points along the Wealdway. There is a 360 degree panorama to delight the walker who finally tops this hill. There is the arc of the sea, the moulding of the green Downs, the sweep of low ground in the north-west, the spread of urban development like a toytown below; and a huge open sky. There are flowers at your feet and birds singing all around. There is space to breathe and at last the knowledge that journey's end is not far off. Combe Hill is a place to pause and take it all in. All too soon it will settle as a fond memory. Enjoy it to the full while you're there.

The path now curves round to the south along the spine of the Downs, making for a car park that is clearly seen from Combe Hill. On the way to it you gain a closer view of the sea, and also of East-bourne far below. On reaching the car park at Butts Brow, go through the kissing gate at the right-hand edge of it and take the broad track leading off towards the right around the hillside. In just over half a mile it brings you to the summit of Willingdon Hill (659 feet above sea level). There is a trig point at the top. Beyond this take the track left and follow it as it steadily loses height. A little over half a mile later you pass a circular stone-based pool, then a golf course. When you reach a peculiar brick memorial seat, branch away from the main track and take instead a path leading among bushes and trees for about ¾ mile to emerge onto the A259 Brighton to Eastbourne road beside Beachy Head Youth Hostel. (Grid ref: 588990) This is the official finish of the Wealdway.

Beachy Head Youth Hostel: *A former golf clubhouse tucked against the Downs on the outskirts of Eastbourne. Standard grade, with 40 beds in dormitories. Meals provided, there are also self-catering facilities and a store in the hostel. Hot showers; camping permissible in the grounds. See the current YHA Guide for up to date information on opening dates and times, and also for present charges. Telephone: Eastbourne (0323) 21081.*

Note: *For those who wish to terminate the walk here, rather than continue for a further couple of miles to Beachy Head proper, turn left on the road and walk downhill into Eastbourne where there are hotels, guest houses, shops, cafés and railway station.*

To continue to Beachy Head, cross the road and turn right. Follow the road uphill until you come level with the golf club car park. The road curves to the right, but leave it and take the footpath heading left. There is a marker post. Keep along this track heading towards the sea. Where the track forks, with two stone markers, take the right fork to pass to the right of a trig point with another circular stone-based pool and two seats just beyond. Bear right along the track, then go left on a path towards trees. Follow this path until it brings you out at a road junction. Cross between these roads and head half-left over the grass to follow a line of gorse bushes up the slope.

Continue in the same direction, following the line of the South Downs Way,(4) with the road running parallel off to the right. The path brings you to the very point of Beachy Head with its plunging cliffs dropping to the surf where the lighthouse braves all weathers. A fitting end to our long walk.

Note: *On the roadside at Beachy Head there is a public telephone kiosk, a café, pub and bus stop to aid a return to Eastbourne. Alternatively, return to Eastbourne by way of the footpath from Beachy Head Youth Hostel, or by a series of cliff paths that give continuing views over the sea.*

Things Seen On The Way:

1. *The Long Man of Wilmington* is England's largest chalk figure. He stands 226 feet in length, naked on the hillside with a stave in each hand, gazing out to the north. There are many theories as to its meaning, and while no-one really knows how old he is, there is some support for his being a product of the Bronze Age. In 1873 the figure was outlined in yellow bricks, but in 1969 these were replaced by white blocks for greater impact and to protect the otherwise exposed chalk. The Long Man is now the property of the Sussex Archaeological Trust who also look after the remains of Wilmington Priory.

2. *Jevington.* Once the haunt of smugglers coming inland from Burling Gap near Beachy Head, Jevington is a small village with some picturesque corners. Like Arlington, it has a Saxon church with Roman bricks used in its construction. Authorities tell us that the Romans brought a road through here from Polegate.

3. *Combe Hill* above Jevington on the South Downs. In the New Stone Age the Downs of southern England were settled by groups of immigrant farmers who created enclosures of small parcels of land in which they experimented with the growing of grain. Unlike the hillforts of the Iron Age, these 'causewayed camps' were not used for defensive purposes, but rather as meeting places for religious cere-

monies, or for trade, as well as for simple farming. Combe Hill is one of these, but it was also later used by Bronze Age man, in about 1500 BC, as a place for the burial of their dead. Burial mounds, or *tumuli*, are seen within the same camp circle.

4. *South Downs Way.* The last of the long-distance routes met on the path of the Wealdway, this stretches for 80 miles between Eastbourne and Buriton and is one of the most popular of all long walks.

Public Transport On Section 6:

Wilmington details are given at the end of Section 5.
Jevington has an infrequent Southdown bus service to Easbourne.
Eastbourne is well served with public transport; both by Southdown buses to various other coastal towns as well as inland to and from a number of places visited by the Wealdway. As for trains, the British Rail station has regular fast services to East Croydon and London; also to Lewes, Hastings and Brighton.

Beachy Head - journey's end for the Wealdway

Oxted Downs on the Vanguard Way

The Vanguard Way

The Vanguard Way

Background

LONG-DISTANCE footpaths grow from many diverse beginnings. Some are 'officially approved' products of the Countryside Commission; some, like the Wealdway, are inspired by the enthusiasm of members of the Ramblers' Association. The Vanguard Way, however, belongs to a comparatively small group of walkers based in Croydon and known as the Vanguards Rambling Club.

Their route runs from East Croydon to Seaford Head; 62 miles long and a linking of existing rights-of-way with short sections of minor roadways. Where the route crosses Ashdown Forest, the Vanguards sought the co-operation of the Conservators of the Forest and, with their help, created a route by adopting publicly accessible rides and tracks that are not, however, actual rights-of-way, but are nevertheless freely accessible. Thus the Vanguard Way now forms a continuous line from the frenetic bustle of London's suburbs to the bracing air of the sea.

Members of the Vanguards Rambling Club were mostly members, too, of the Youth Hostels Association, and when they were planning their route, many were the nights they spent at my hostel, Crockham Hill, discussing the merits of certain field or woodland routes over other suggestions. I watched, amused at times by their enthusiastic approach, and admired the thoroughness with which they tackled the project.

In 1980 as a celebration of the 15th anniversary of the founding of the Vanguards Rambling Club, conveniently timed to coincide with the Golden Jubilee of the YHA and the Ramblers' Association's own 'Footpath Heritage '80', the Vanguard Way was established; a fitting way to mark any one of these celebrations, and a worthy tribute to the hard work of a few dedicated walkers.

The Vanguards produced their own route guide in 1980, and I should like here to openly acknowledge the quite splendid job they made of it, too. It is one of the most accurate footpath guides I have ever used. Inevitably, small sections have become a little out of date by now, but it is still a remarkable achievement that is worth seeking out. I salute all those involved in its production and offer this guide, not to compete with it, but to complement it.

The Route

BREAKING free of Croydon's tower blocks and traffic, the Vanguard Way is soon among woodlands and meadows. It passes through

Selsdon Woods Nature Reserve and takes to the fields that form part of the North Downs escarpment, leading then to the hamlet of Farleigh. From there through more woods, out to Chelsham Common and meandering over the back of the Downs above Woldingham. Up there it's a broad open country with huge skies, but a sudden drop takes the walker into a tight little valley, to climb out again straight after and gradually heading towards the very edge of the North Downs where a dramatic view opens to the west.

The Vanguard Way crosses the North Downs Way at Titsey; it goes over the M25 motorway and along a lane to the edge of Westerham before dipping into fine woods that climb onto the Greensand Ridge. Here, at Limpsfield Chart, the Greensand Way is crossed, and a moment later the route plunges over the southern lip of the ridge along a track that bore a literary pilgrimage in the years at the turn of the century.

Ahead lies the Weald. Vast views look across to another ridge, and beyond that to the hint of Ashdown Forest. This is a wide and lovely country, the more surprising for its comparatively close proximity to London. Crockham Hill lies here, the end of the first section, but continuing, the walker is led deeper into the Weald's low pastures. Haxted Mill, a lovely old watermill now turned into a museum and restaurant, is on the route. Then fields again; it goes alongside the former Starborough Castle before a long steady climb leads to a hillside of orchards with more wonderful panoramas out to the north. On the top of Dry Hill, Iron Age man made his campment. The Weald was spread out at his feet.

South of Dry Hill a stretch of quiet road walking brings the Vanguard Way to a delightful series of field and woodland paths, through a neat parkland and more fields with peaceful views, before coming into the pleasant little town of Forest Row.

Forest Row is on the edge of Ashdown Forest. The route now climbs over this heathland, touches Newbridge with its stream ford, then goes up to the lofty belvedere near Gills Lap Clump from which point you can see back across the Greensand hills to the North Downs in the distance. Then it's a case of heading into open Forest again, along a superb spine of a slope with the South Downs now seen far off. The Forest is left behind and traded for meadows once more. One of the most delightful of sections leads to the tiny hamlet of High Hurstwood in rolling country of great charm. Past this hamlet with its lovely church, then across more fields and onto another lane. An agricultural landscape, easy on the eye, pleasant under foot, ever interesting, it takes the route eventually to a chance meeting with the

East Croydon tower blocks seen from Vanguard Way near Coombe Woods

Wealdway at Tickerage Mill on the outskirts of Blackboys.

South of Blackboys the route plunges again into agricultural countryside. For a while it runs parallel with the Wealdway, several fields away but keeping to the east of East Hoathly before crossing the Wealdway once again, this time in the village of Chiddingly. The church here is worth visiting as you pass through. Beyond Chiddingly a large meadow leads to a wood, and from the wood across fields working ever southward into the low land that forms such a contrast to the South Downs that it gradually leads to. There's another lane to follow, a track through woods and out to a farmland where the Downs loom large ahead.

Having crossed a number of low fields and streams, the way climbs into Berwick village and over an interesting whale-backed hill to drop into one of the finest of all Sussex villages, Alfriston.

Alfriston overlooks the Cuckmere, and the Vanguard Way now follows this river, sometimes beside it, sometimes on the Downs above, all the way to the sea. On the Downs the way coincides with the South Downs Way. It works a route through Friston Forest and comes out to a lovely view of Cuckmere Haven with the river winding in ox-bows below.

Crossing the river by way of Exceat Bridge, the route now heads along the right bank of the river, through Seaford Head Nature Reserve to the opening of Cuckmere Haven where the glorious Seven Sisters cliffs rear majestically across the estuary. The Vanguard Way turns its back on these cliffs and climbs its own up to Seaford Head. There, on a seat with a view, the Vanguard Way reaches it worthy finale.

SECTION 1: EAST CROYDON TO CROCKHAM HILL

Distance:	15 miles
Map:	O.S. Landranger series; Sheet 177 *East London Area*; Sheet 187 *Dorking, Reigate and Crawley* 1:50,000
Accommodation:	Croydon - Hotels and guest houses Crockham Hill - Youth Hostel Elsewhere - hotels, b&b in Westerham (1¾ miles off-route to the north of Crockham Hill), and hotels in Edenbridge (2½ miles south of Crockham Hill).

On leaving the railway station at East Croydon the walker is confronted by a vision of nose-to-tail traffic, scurrying commuters and towering modern office blocks. Hardly a country lover's skyline, it's a landscape of concrete and glass. However, before long these are traded for the quiet of parks, the birdsong of woodlands and the open vistas of the North Downs. The transformation is welcome. It is a gentle introduction to the ever varied South and one that comes as something of a surprise to those who may previously have thought that London stretched to the sea.

From the North Downs the Vanguard Way drops down to cross the M25, London's orbital motorway, then immediately climbs south onto the lovely wooded Greensand Ridge. From the lip of this ridge a huge panorama opens across the lush pastures and fields of the Weald to the blue rise of the distant Ashdown Forest and the hint of many delights yet to come.

This first day's introduction makes an enjoyable outing and eases the walker gently into the pleasures of the hospitable English countryside where variety is the order of the day.

Outside East Croydon's station bear left and use the underpass which goes beneath the main road and leads to Altyre Road. Walk along this and turn right at the end to reach a zebra crossing. Over this, go right, then left straight away onto Fairfield Path. This a route that leads through a residential area. Follow Fairfield Path along to Stanhope Road, which you cross with a school on your right, and go straight ahead to a T road junction. At this point turn right, and a few yards later cross the road and continue along Fairfield Path as it goes among some new houses. Soon the path drops down to another road, which you cross at a pedestrian crossing. Turn right and take the path as it bears left about 15 yards further on. This rises to reach another road among more new houses. Bear right and follow this past the houses to

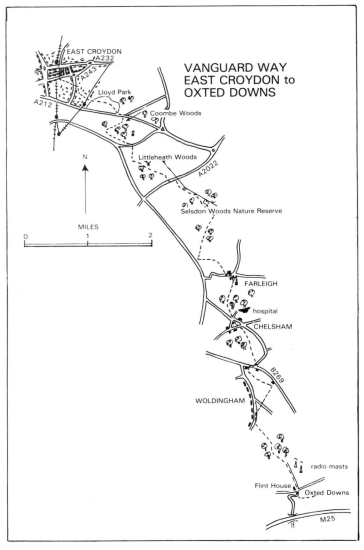

find the continuing Fairfield Path as it cuts beside house number 1. The path leads to Brownlow Road, crosses it and continues in the same direction to duck beneath a railway bridge. Beyond lies Lloyd Park.

Croydon's commercial centre has been left behind. Ahead is a stretch of grassland with clumps of trees and a breath of the country.

Cross the road and bear left along the fence of a bowling green. Turn right at the end of the fence and follow it along its second side. Then cut across the park, continuing in the same direction towards a spinney of large trees. As you draw near you will notice there are children's swings and seesaws there. Leaving the children's play area bear half-right to gain the road that runs alongside the park, then go left beside the road for about 300 yards until you reach Conduit Lane on the opposite side of the road. Cross the road with care and enter Conduit Lane.

Coombe Woods Centre, which lies on the left of the lane, is a blaze of colour in spring and early summer. A pool in the corner near the road adds a touch of character. There are shrubs beyond; gardens, flowers and many fine trees. Refreshments are available in a café there. Croydon suddenly seems a long way off.

Walk along Conduit Lane, go beyond a barrier and bear right after 40 yards along a track, muddied by horses, that goes between fences. There are woods overhanging the track, with birds and squirrels to watch as you pass beneath. The track descends in the woods after a surprise view off to the right that shows Croydon's tower blocks not so far away. When the track reaches the garage of a house, turn left and follow as the route leads along the edge of woods towards Addington. The track comes to a road, at which point turn right, cross it and 50 yards later go left into a residential street, Crest Road. This reaches Croham Valley Road. Cross this and continue along an enclosed footpath for 40 yards where you then turn left on a path leading to Littleheath Woods.

On a bright May morning, Littleheath Woods were filled with joint pleasures of bluebells and birdsong. Badger setts were scratched at their entrances to indicate recent activity. There was a fresh smell of earth and damp foliage; new leaves were silken to the touch. There were squirrels scampering up trees all about me. A cuckoo called far off. In the woods there's a confusion of paths, but a line of silver skeleton pylons pointed me in the right direction. Apart from these, it was real country at least.

Go into the woods. Ignore the first track on the right, but 20 yards further on veer right and climb uphill among trees. Continue along this path to the top of the hill and descend on the far side, crossing a major track towards an open meadow. Keeping the meadow on your left take the path directly ahead as it climbs uphill again in woods. A water tower is seen at the top of this hill, half hidden by trees to the left of the path. Pass beyond it, over a broad trail, heading towards houses, then some 20 yards after crossing the main track, find a smaller path that leads downhill and follows along the line of gardens seen to the right. The path brings you out into a residential street. Turn left and follow along this to reach the busy Selsdon Park Road. (Grid ref: 358627)

At this main road bear left for a few yards until you reach the entrance to Ashen Vale on the other side. With caution cross the road and turn into Ashen Vale, signposted here to Yew Tree Way. Take the footpath as it leads through the recent housing development, rising at the end to the fenced area of Selsdon Woods Nature Reserve.(1) Go through the gate, turn right and a few yards later head left, climbing uphill on a clear path into the woods.

The path cuts straight through the Reserve. There are other paths, but the Vanguard Way insists on maintaining its direct line. Beside the path will be found wood anemones early in the year, then bluebells. The path leads to another metal gate. Go through it, leaving the Reserve behind, and turn right to take the left-hand of two tracks. This leads to yet more woods. Follow the path all the way. Out of the woods it becomes a sunken track bounded by overhanging trees and hedges, a bridle path that is often muddy in places. It comes to a lay-by with all the attendant litter that is one of the shameful faces of our land and modern society.

Turn left here, cross a stile signposted to Farleigh Court, and go along the right-hand edge of a field. The path touches another wood, then edges alongside it on a track that eventually heads right along a fence towards farm buildings. Follow the track to a road where you turn left, and a few yards later head right into the little hamlet of Farleigh. There's nothing much to it, except one or two farms, a few houses and a lovely old church dating back to about 1083.

You reach the church of St. Mary's and, keeping it on your left, take the bridle path that goes straight ahead between fields to a wood. Enter the wood, bear right and follow the main track as it goes through - muddy in places - but on emerging from it go left through barriers on a sometimes overgrown path. This leads between fences and comes to a road opposite Woldingham Park School. Cross the

*The Vanguard Way climbing through Littleheath Woods
outside Croydon*

road and bear half-right to go over the common ahead. Pass The Bull pub on your left and turn left to follow the hedge that runs alongside Chelsham Common. A path leads to a pond half-circled with trees. A quiet place for a picnic.

Go round the right-hand side of the pond and cut across to reach the road. Just before you come to crossroads, head right along a track. This brings you to a large field with a wood bordering it. Go along the right-hand edge of the field, then after half a mile go through trees to come onto another road. Turn right here and follow the road to its junction with the B269. Turn right again for about 40 yards, then cross over to pick up a somewhat tangled path marked by a metal sign and a stone, the latter may be hidden by long grass. (Grid ref: 375579) The path leads alongside the fence of Lodge Cottage and once more into woodlands. It becomes a little confusing, but the direction to take is straight ahead. The path becomes more obvious after a few yards and leads out of the wood again by way of a stile into a field. Maintain the same direction to pass a curious deep hollow on the right, then make towards the fence of a cottage seen across the open field.

Here on the Downs there's a sense of space. Huge skies create cloudscapes as interesting as the countryside through which you walk.

At its right-hand corner the cottage fence meets a hedge. Follow the hedge downhill with lovely views into the combe below and far off where London bids farewell. It's a steep descent that can be treacherous after rain. There are two or three stiles to cross, and at the bottom of the hill the route continues straight ahead to climb the far side. More stiles. With a hedge on the left go over the crown of this hill and drop down to a road lined on one side by the houses of Woldingham.

Turn left and walk along the road until it curves to the right. At this point leave the road and take the broad bridle path seen heading uphill towards woodlands. Enter the woods by a gate and continue along the track. When it comes out of the woods there's a splendid rolling parkland off to the right, all green and lush with folding hills and vales below. The bridle path eventually brings you onto a road beside Flint House. Cross the road to take the narrow descending lane opposite. After a little under 100 yards take the footpath going ahead through trees - the road here bears right - and a moment or two later a surprise view opens out. (Grid ref: 387545)

The Downs plunged away and through the valley below roared the traffic of the M25, but my eyes were drawn along the line of the North Downs

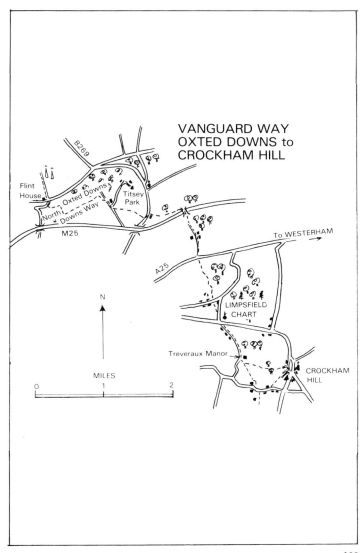

VANGUARD WAY
OXTED DOWNS to
CROCKHAM HILL

B269

Flint
House

North Oxted Downs
Downs Way

Titsey
Park

M25

A25

To WESTERHAM

N

LIMPSFIELD
CHART

Treveraux Manor

CROCKHAM
HILL

MILES

0   1   2

easing out to the west with jutting spurs green with beeches, and far beyond, line upon line of hills fading blue until their shapes mingled with the sky. Then across the valley to a saddle in the Greensand Ridge. Woods and yet more woodlands and the huge expanse of the Weald showing as a hinted plain off in the south. Across the snaking concrete motorway lay the toytown houses of Oxted and Limpsfield. This is country the Romans knew well, and I wondered for a moment how this landscape would have appeared to them, nearly two thousand years ago and hundreds of miles from the sun-baked plains of Italy. To me, this was a homely landscape. I cursed the need for motorways, but revelled in the glory of hill and valley and mighty beech crowns that gave to the Downs additional height and authority.

Bear left and follow the fence along the edge of the hill until you reach a stile on your right. Cross this and descend steeply, taking great care if the grass is wet. At the bottom of the slope you come to a fence with a path running along the side of it. This is the North Downs Way.(2) Turn left and follow this path towards Titsey Woods. Keeping the woods on your left, a series of stiles leads the path along the headland of one or two large fields. Eventually the path is confronted by a line of trees running downhill from the woods. The path goes into these and drops onto a sunken lane. Here the Vanguard Way parts company with the North Downs Way. Turn right and follow the sunken lane to a farm. Along this lane various footpath waymarks(3) will be seen. Ignore them all and continue on the main track.

Near the farm the lane becomes a narrow road. Go beyond the entrance to Titsey Park and take the bridle path which leaves the road to the left. After about 30 yards cross a stile seen on your left and enter a field. Here bear half-right to cross the field and make for a trackway in the far corner leading into another field. There's a small stream here. Cross through a gate into the next field and follow the line of stiles linking several more fields, to reach a little footbridge over a stream with the B269 road beyond. Turn left on the road and walk along it for 100 yards. Leave the road by a stile on the right immediately after you pass a waterworks building, and follow the line of a fence into the field. Beyond the fence continue in the same direction towards the motorway. Now bear left along the side of a wooden fence until it brings you to a bridge leading over the motorway.

Cross the bridge and the motorway. Happily the sound of traffic is soon lost on the broad track that leads beside yet more woodlands to Broomlands Farm. On reaching the farm the track becomes a road. It

Greensand country near Crockham Hill

is essential to exercise great caution through the farm as heavy lorries trundle back and forth when working in the huge sand pit seen off to the right.

Take the road uphill beyond Broomlands Farm until you come to the A25 road at Moorhouse Bank. (Grid ref: 421522)

Note: *Walkers wishing to find overnight accommodation in Westerham; or any using this as a day's walk from Croydon and planning to return by bus, should leave the Vanguard Way here. Turn left and walk along the A25 for 1¾ miles to Westerham. In Westerham there are also refreshments, public toilets and telephone kiosks. Places of interest include Quebec House and Squerryes Court.*

Cross the A25 and follow the bridle path opposite. Go through a metal gate and head directly across a large field to reach a wood. The London Countryway(4) crosses at this point. Enter the wood and aim half-right among the trees on a path that skirts along the right-hand edge of it. Keeping on this path you will be led to a road with the houses of Limpsfield Chart beyond. Cross over the road and wander along the edge of a cricket pitch with the woods behind it, to reach another road. (To the right, a short diversion brings you to The Carpenters Arms, for those in need of liquid refreshment.) The Vanguard Way goes straight ahead, passing the route of the Greensand Way(5) and in front of St. Andrew's Church on the left.

The Vanguard Way below Trevereaux Hill, near Crockham Hill

Just beyond the church cross another road. This is yet again the B269. Take the track beyond with a few houses on the right. A little way along this driveway you come to the lip of the Greensand Ridge and there are spectacular views off to the right - seen at their best across the walled garden of a house. The surface of the driveway deteriorates as it loses height down the southern slope of the hill. This is Trevereaux Hill.(6)

At the foot of the hill the track reaches Trevereaux Manor with its little gold dome on the roof. Keep to the track as it bears right past the entrance to the Manor, and shortly after, with a pair of cottages on your right, find a stile in the hedge to the left. Cross this and enter a large flat field with broad views of the meadows of the Weald, and some interesting hills to the south. Here the Vanguard Way divides. For those intending to stay overnight in Crockham Hill, follow Alternative Route 1, otherwise follow Alternative 2, the original route.

Alternative Route 1:
Bear left along the fence that runs in front of Trevereaux Manor, and where it changes direction keep straight ahead, making for a gate in

the hedgerow across the field. A stile to the left side of the gate crosses into the next field. Here you pass out of Surrey and into Kent. Cross this first Kentish field along its left-hand side beside a ditch and a hedge, and at the far side cross another stile and over a stream on stepping stones. Take the path leading uphill into trees, and on emerging from them cross yet another stile into a sloping field with houses at the top. Keep to the left of this field and come onto a lane by way of an awkward stile beside the boundary of the left-hand house. You are now in Oakdale Lane.

Turning to admire the view a vast panorama is laid out for your enjoyment as you gaze along the Greensand Ridge to the North Downs far off; a lovely vista of hill and valley, of woodland and meadow. At all times of the year it threatens to delay the walker with its vision of countless acres of sheer enchantment. There are woodpeckers in the spinney below. Nightingales may sometimes be heard there; there are rabbits in the meadows and foxes in the copse. Larks hang as tiny specks in a huge sky, trilling fit to bust. Sheep bleat in a distant pasture. It's a landscape matured and tended and specifically laid out, it would seem, for the benefit of the people fortunate enough to live here. It's fortunate too for the walker to have accessible paths leading through it. One of many good things to enjoy along the way.

Turn right and walk along Oakdale Lane, past cottages and a converted oast house, to reach another road. Here turn right and so come in 50 yards to the main road. On reaching this you'll find a Post Office Stores opposite, and a public telephone kiosk 50 yards further downhill directly opposite the Royal Oak pub. Turning right along the main road follow down for about 150 yards to find the Youth Hostel standing on the right behind white gates.

Crockham Hill Youth Hostel: *A large Victorian house standing in more than two acres of grounds. Standard grade, with 47 beds in dormitories. Hot showers, meals provided, self-cookers' kitchen, small store, drying facilities. Camping permissible in the gounds. See the current YHA Guide for up-to-date information on opening dates and times, and also for present charges. Telephone: Edenbridge (0732) 866322.*

Crockham Hill sits on the southern slopes of the Greensand Ridge. A small village, it is noted for its magnificent views and for Chartwell, former home of Sir Winston Churchill, which lies 1½ miles away over Mariners Hill. There is much National Trust property in and around the village, and one of the co-founders of the Trust, Octavia Hill, lived for part of her life in a house she had built on the edge of Crockham Hill Common. When she died it was her wish to be buried in the churchyard here, and in the church of the Holy Trinity there is a marble effigy lying beside the altar. Her grave is beneath a large yew immediately at the top of the entrance steps of the churchyard, on the right.

Alternative Route 2:

This avoids the detour to Crockham Hill. Go half-right into the field in front of Trevereaux Manor, and walk towards a large tree that stands beside a pond. Maintain more or less the same direction and cross the field towards a distant cottage with an oast house seen behind it. There's a small gate in the hedgerow, with a plank bridge over a ditch. Cross into the next field and continue in the same direction, making for the near corner of a fence around a paddock behind the cottage. On reaching the fence bear left along it. At its end cross a stile to the right, then out of the paddock by way of another stile beside a field gate, so to come onto a lane. This is Dairy Lane. Go ahead along this lane, passing in a few yards the entrance to Hurst Farm on your right. About 100 yards beyond this you'll find the entrance to Dairy Green, a house seen at the top of a drive. Here the route from Crockham Hill (Alternative Route 1) rejoins the Vanguard Way.

Things Seen On The Way:

1. *Selsdon Woods Nature Reserve*, on the edge of a large housing development, is a fenced area of woodland in the hands of the National Trust since 1935. Now administered by the Parks Department of the London Borough of Croydon, there are some 200 acres of woodland in all. Typical woodland flower species.

2. *North Downs Way.* One of the best known of the long distance walking routes in the south, much of the route is combined with the Pilgrims Way. The North Downs Way is about 141 miles in length from Farnham to Dover.

3. *Titsey Foundation Walk.* On the edge of the North Downs the Vanguard Way goes through a portion of Titsey Park. On the way a number of waymarks are seen. These refer to the Titsey Foundation Walk; a fine outing that explores the woods and hillsides of the Park, in which the remains of a Roman villa were discovered in the 19th century.

4. *London Countryway.* This long distance walk is a 205 mile circuit of the capital. Constables publish a route guide written by the instigator of the walk, Keith Chesterton.

5. *Greensand Way.* Yet another long distance walking route, this has yet to be completed. The aim is to have a continuous route leading from Haslemere in Surrey to Hythe in Kent. For several years the route has been made and waymarked through Surrey, from Haslemere to the Surrey/Kent boundary above Crockham Hill, totalling 55 miles. Recently (1986) the 20 miles of the West Kent section from Crockham Hill to Yalding has been opened, thereby giving 75 miles of magnificent walking. When completed the Greensand Way promises to be one of the most scenically spectacular long walks in the south.

6. *Trevereaux Hill* not only grants lovely views over a wide landscape, it is the site of a one-time literary pilgrimage. In the late 19th and early 20th century, there lived in the nearby woods Edward and Constance Garnett; he an influential publisher's reader, she a noted translator of the Russian classics. Such was their standing that many of the great writers of the day came here to spend time in their company. Thus today's walker follows where Conrad and Wells and Galsworthy, Hudson, Thomas and Lawrence and many more walked and found inspiration. Near the foot of the hill there's a pond where W.H.Hudson discovered natterjack toads, and all around are scenes from various novels woven in landscapes of great beauty.

Public Transport On Section 1:

East Croydon is well served by bus from many parts of Central London, Kent and Surrey. Also main line railway station linking London (Victoria and London Bridge), Redhill, Gatwick Airport, East Grinstead, Haywards Heath, Brighton etc.
Westerham has London Country bus links with Croydon, Bromley etc.
Limpsfield Chart has infrequent daily buses (LC), not Sundays, to Oxted for British Rail link with London and East Croydon.
Crockham Hill has no public transport facilities of use to Vanguard Way walkers.

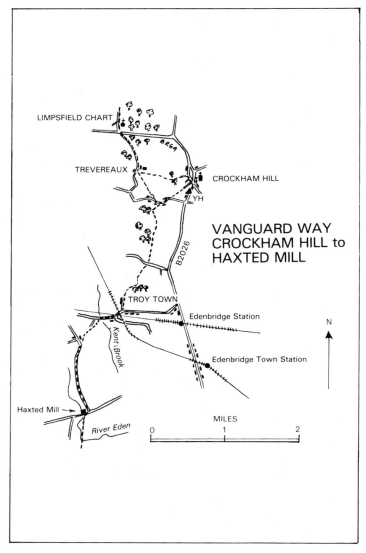

LIMPSFIELD CHART

TREVEREAUX

CROCKHAM HILL

YH

B269

B2026

**VANGUARD WAY
CROCKHAM HILL to
HAXTED MILL**

TROY TOWN

Edenbridge Station

Edenbridge Town Station

Kent Brook

N

Haxted Mill

River Eden

MILES

0   1   2

SECTION 2: CROCKHAM HILL TO FOREST ROW

Distance:	13 miles
Map:	O.S. Landranger series; Sheet 187 *Dorking, Reigate and Crawley* 1:50,000
Accommodation:	Forest Row - hotels, b&b

The main feature of this section of the walk is the crossing of Dry Hill, the site of an Iron Age encampment. It's a lofty eminence that commands some of the finest views of the whole walk. Before reaching that, however, there is a stretch of low valley walking often on soggy Wealden clay. Fortunately there is always plenty of interest along this part, too. After Dry Hill the way switches over wooded ridges in a lively set of enclosed landscapes before coming to the rather pleasant little town of Forest Row on the edge of Ashdown Forest.

Taken leisurely, with an eye on the country, there will be time to sniff the breeze and to listen to the birds. Actual walking time to Forest Row will be around 5 to 5½ hours, while fast and determined walkers could continue as far as Blackboys to make a full 10 hour day of it; but far better to take the walk in all its variety without an eye on the clock.

Alternative Route: (From Crockham Hill Youth Hostel)
On leaving the Youth Hostel turn left at the gate and walk back along the main road to take the first road left after The Royal Oak. This is Deanery Road, a residential street. Go down to the end of this road to find a bridle path between the last of the houses and the last of the bungalows. The track has a fence to the left and a hedgerow to the right. It passes through a gateway and enters a large field with views ahead to a long ridge whose highest point is Dry Hill, over which the Vanguard Way will lead. Beyond this ridge can be seen another. This is Ashdown Forest. Between the two ridges lies Forest Row.

Go down the right-hand edge of this field to its end where you come onto a lane; Dairy Lane. Bear right and follow this lane straight ahead. About 100 yards along this, notice the very fine Old Dairy Farm(1) on the left, standing back across a neat lawn with a pond on the corner. The lane curves to the right and a few yards later you will come to the entrance of Dairy Green, there to rejoin the Vanguard Way proper.

Vanguard Way Continued Route:
Head up Dairy Green drive for a few yards until you come to a stile on the left. Over this bear right and follow up the slope between wire fences. At the top left-hand corner of this narrow field cross another

117

stile to the left and follow along the headland of this field with a fence to your right. A third stile leads out of this field and into another. Turn right to go along the edge of the field, over another stile by a pond, then over another stile to the corner of a large wood. Continue ahead, still in the same direction, following beside Guildables Wood. The path crosses another stile and along another field with the wood on your right still. When the wood finishes, go straight ahead up the gentle slope of the field to locate a stile to the left of an oak tree. Crossing this you come onto a lane. (Grid ref: 432488)

Turn left for 40 yards, then go through a gate on the right, marked by a stone footpath sign. The route now lies along the left-hand edge of two fields with good views over folding meadowland off to the right, and also looking back towards the Greensand Ridge. Having reached the end of the second field, turn right and walk along the edge of it with a hedge on your left. When you come in view of some cottages and a fine old barn ahead to the left, go out of the field by way of a metal gate to pass in front of the cottages along a lane. This small collection of buildings rejoices in the name of Troy Town. Continue along this lane until it reaches a T junction, at which point go right.

Note: *Walkers planning to stay overnight in Edenbridge, having extended Section 1, will leave the route here. They, and any who might wish to return to East Croydon by train, should go left here and follow the lane for about a mile. When it reaches a main road turn right and follow this into Edenbridge. Hotel accommodation will be found along the main road. Prospective train travellers to East Croydon should note that Edenbridge Town station is closed on Sundays. However, the first station met along the main road - Edenbridge station - although little more than a halt, has a daily service of trains between Tonbridge and Redhill, where connections may be made for London.*

Follow the road as it winds over a crossing of railway lines on a bridge, and at the next junction turn right again. The road slopes downhill with one or two houses beside it. At the bottom of the hill it crosses a stream known as Kent Brook, for here runs the boundary between Kent and Surrey. Across the stream two footpath signs point off to the left. Take the second of these routes, next to a farm entrance, and cross the field, over two stiles and into the next field. Crossing this there may not be any visible sign of a path on the ground; but make for a stile to the left of a line of trees and pass into the next field. On the far side leave the field by way of a gate in the left-hand corner, then turn right and follow the line of a wire fence which will lead out by way of another stile onto a road near farm buildings. This is Shinglebarn Farm. Opposite runs the approach drive to Wintersell Farm. Turn left and walk along the road for a mile, then bear right at the next junction.

It was early still as I headed along the road with the banks shoulder high with cow parsley, and I peered up at the morning sky through a frieze of minute white starry flowers to gain the perspective of hedgerow creatures. Yellow archangel exploited the lower slope of hedgerows and bluebells painted a smokey haze among clumps of trees. It may not have been quite like meadow walking, nor with the obvious pleasures of wandering through woods, but there is something of interest wherever you look, and I counted birds' nests in the hedges, peered through gateways at meadows with streams winding through them, listened to birdsong and the scampering, unseen, of mice or voles through the grass and leaves that bordered the road. There was so much to absorb that I forgot the tarmac, and it came as something of a surprise to find that the mile had been walked and it was only a short stroll now down to Haxted Mill.

Having turned right at the road junction, the road drops down in a curve and comes to the lovely white weather boarded Haxted Mill.(2) On the left, opposite the watermill and immediately before the bridge over the Eden, cross the stile into a field and walk through it, keeping a hedge to your left. The stream winds lazily through the field to your right, but then the path crosses a small bridge over it, and goes straight ahead to reach a narrow country road by way of a metal gate. Here turn left and follow the road, over a bridge, to a fork. Take the left fork for about 400 yards until the road makes a sharp right-hand turn. Directly ahead you'll find a stile. Cross this into the field ahead, but bear left round a hedge and follow this to the end of the field, then a short distance left again to find a gap allowing access to the next field. (There should be a stile, but this was missing at the time of writing.) Through the gap turn right and walk alongside the hedgerow for 30 yards before heading directly across the field to a stile with a pond on its left. Over the stile turn right along a track by Cernes Farm. (Grid ref: 426445)

The track becomes a metalled drive. Turn right along this drive with railings on your left, as far as a stile found on the left. Cross the stile, go through the metal gate beyond and, keeping a hedge on your left, find another stile which leads onto the drive of Starborough Castle.(3) Turn right and wander along the drive through an avenue of shady trees.

Hackstead Mill, now a watermill museum on the Vanguard Way

The drive from Starborough Castle reaches the B2028 road. Turn
right and walk along it for 150 yards, then cross over and take the
bridle path which heads away to the left immediately before a house.
This bridle path leads through some rather pleasant country. It strikes
along the right-hand side of two or three fields, becomes an enclosed
track and then reaches another track near a cottage seen a short
distance off to your right. Bear right along this new track, then a few
yards later turn left through a gate and follow the bridle path as it
climbs uphill. There are growing views left into the low country of the
Weald, with the bank of the Greensand Ridge on the far side. The
track leads into a wood, now losing the views, but replacing them with
more birdsong and shade loving flowers. The track becomes a path
and enters an orchard. Keep along the left-hand edge of the orchard
with the wood now to one side. As you work your way higher beside
the rows of fruit trees, so the views begin once more to open out. On
reaching a broad track by a house, turn right towards farm buildings.
(This is Dry Hill fruit farm, and in the season there's plenty of pick-
your own fruit to be had here. Perhaps you'll be tempted to make a
short diversion to buy a pound of strawberries for your lunch!) As you

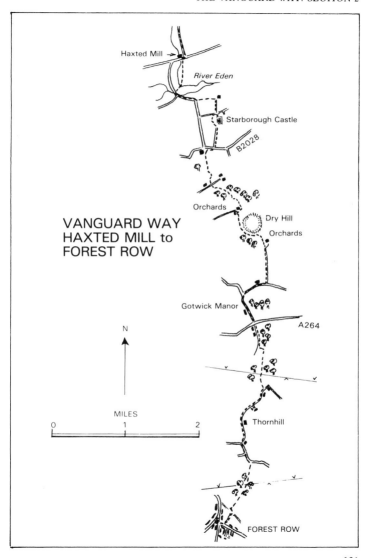

Haxted Mill →

River Eden

Starborough Castle

B2028

Orchards

Dry Hill

Orchards

VANGUARD WAY
HAXTED MILL to
FOREST ROW

Gotwick Manor

A264

N

MILES

0   1   2

Thornhill

FOREST ROW

Orchard at Dry Hill, looking north into The Weald -
Greensand Ridge in distance

come to the farm buildings turn left again to head uphill; but before
doing so, go right for a moment and enjoy the huge vista spread out
before you.

*I struck it lucky, for the air was filled with apple blossom. Bees were
thundering in their masses from one lavish cluster of flowers to another.
Through the orchard avenues washed a fragrance brought by the warm
spring morning. But beyond, the land eased away and all the Weald, it
seemed, lay before me. The view was to the north, and it encompassed all
the morning's walk and half of yesterday's too. For beyond the broad valley
rose the Greensand hills, and over them, making a blue line, ran the North
Downs. It seemed impossible to believe that London lay just beyond that
horizon of splendour.*

Go uphill on the farm track, ignoring others that branch from it,
and so reach the brow of the hill with its crown of trees. This is Dry
Hill Fort,(4) site of an Iron Age encampment dating from about 500
BC. Once again the views are magnificent, especially those looking to

the right (west) into the last of Surrey and the first of Sussex.

From the entrance to Dry Hill Fort bear right on a track that runs along the edge of an orchard, go through a gate on the right and descend south through a second orchard, forking right and following a line of trees on your left to reach a gate. The gate leads to another track. Follow this ahead, soon to see a pond on your left and a neat farm ahead; this makes a pretty scene with a wooded landscape ahead across a folding of meadows. Turn left on reaching a dutch barn, and on a farm track go right and follow this for little over half a mile down to a quiet country road. Here turn right and pass a lovely house on a bend in the road, and a quarter of a mile farther along you come to a road junction. Turn left, plunging downhill between hedges, crossing a stream at the bottom and entering East Sussex. The road climbs again with a wood on the left and Gotwick Manor on the right; and so to reach the busy A264 East Grinstead to Tunbridge Wells road.

Cross the main road and take the driveway opposite. In early summer the drive is aflame with rhododendrons. Go down the drive for about 500 yards, and where it bears to the right at the end of the wood, cut off to the left, through a gate and into a field. The path leads alongside the edge of the wood, then through a metal gate where you turn right through another field. You now go along the right-hand side of two more fields until you reach a wooden gate leading into a wood. Go straight ahead on the path through the wood. This is sometimes a little muddy.

Once out of the wood continue directly ahead to pass beneath power lines, climbing uphill now for 400 yards to reach a lane. Here turn right and follow along the lane for about a mile. It takes you through a splendid park-like region and in front of an imposing house, Thornhill. Eventually you come to a T junction by Homefield Cottages. Head left along this lane, and 50 yards later turn right along a rough track. After another 200 yards bear left on a lane and follow along this past Grove Farm Cottages. When the lane bears left, some 200 yards later, head right along a path which leads between two rows of trees; now and then with views off to the right to catch sight of Weir Wood Reservoir trapped in a bowl of wooded hills in the distance.

The path among these trees was a delight. There were bluebells and orchids beside the path; one stile after another leading deeper and deeper into a world of leaf and shade while squirrels darted up the trunks of trees and along branches overhead. Walking alone I heard sounds that are too often lost when in company. There was time to pause among the flowers and to catch the fresh scent of damp foliage. From a beech tree a tiny green

Beeches Farm on the southern slopes of Dry Hill

caterpillar dangled on an invisible thread of gossamer, jerking its loose hinged body in a futile attempt to climb back to the branch from which it hung - to the caterpillar, as good as a thousand feet above. I guessed its destiny was to be the lunch of a woodland bird soon after I left.

The footpath leaves the shade of trees, goes through a gate and joins a track by a waterworks building. One hundred yards later the way crosses a metalled track and, going half-right between posts, enters a car park. Head left, then straight away go right to a pavement beside a road that leads directly to the B2110 road and Forest Row.

Forest Row is a pleasant little town set among hills with Ashdown Forest a short stroll away. The town, or perhaps one could call it a large village, has good shopping facilities and several cafés and pubs for refreshment. There are two hotels; Ashdown Forest Golf Hotel in Chapel Lane; and Brambletye Hotel in Lewes Road. Several of the town's buildings are of interest and two of them, Kidbrooke Mansion and Ashdown House are open to the public.

Things Seen On The Way:

1. *Old Dairy Farm*, Crockham Hill, is a lovely old house first mentioned in a Court Roll of 1547. The original Tudor Hall was reduced by the addition of a ceiling some time early in the 18th century in order to create two storeys. It still has a gallery. At the turn of the century it was occupied by a family of Armenian refugees and their bodyguards, but they made themselves so unpopular in the neighbourhood that locals virtually ran them out of the village.

2. *Haxted Mill.* This delightful old watermill dates back to 1680, but occupies the site of an even earlier mill of the 14th century. Here, on the banks of the little River Eden, Haxted Mill functioned well for centuries, until in 1949 it finally ceased commercial milling. Since then it has taken on a new lease of life as a Watermill Museum. Inside you'll find various items of milling machinery and working models. There's an exhibition, too, devoted to the Wealden iron industry. It's a fascinating museum, and if you have time to call in when it is open, I urge you to do so. Refreshments are also available.

3. *Starborough Castle* remains in name only now. The moat can just be seen from the Vanguard Way. History tells us that the Normans built a castle here, and then a later one was built on the site by Lord Cobham. In 1649, after the Civil War, the castle was taken apart and a hundred years later a Gothic house rose on the site.

4. *Dry Hill Fort.* Occupying a magnificent hilltop view over a huge sweep of country, Dry Hill was chosen as an Iron Age encampment about 500 BC, and it covered about 24 acres in all. It is thought that a trackway led between this camp and a similar one on Crockham Hill on the Greensand Ridge, which point can be clearly seen from here. Dry Hill Fort is privately owned, and much of the site is covered by orchard, but paths lead over it.

Public Transport On Section 2:

Edenbridge boasts two railway stations; Edenbridge, which is little more than a halt, is on the Tonbridge-Redhill-Guildford-Reading line and has a daily service. Edenbridge Town station, closed on Sundays, serves the London-East Croydon-Uckfield line.
Forest Row has buses serving East Grinstead (Maidstone and District and Southdown). There are M.&D. buses to Tunbridge Wells; and S.D. to Uckfield.

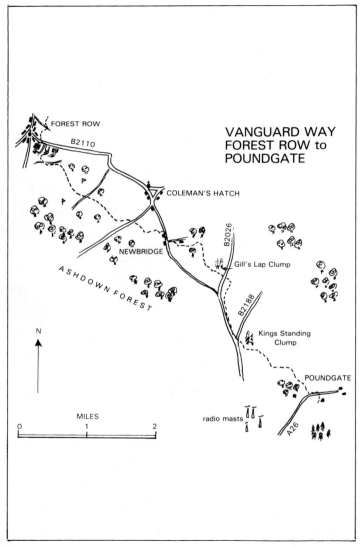

VANGUARD WAY
FOREST ROW to
POUNDGATE

SECTION 3: FOREST ROW TO BLACKBOYS

Distance:	13 miles
Maps:	O.S. Landranger series; Sheets 187 *Dorking, Reigate and Crawley;* Sheet 188 *Maidstone and The Weald of Kent* and Sheet 199 *Eastbourne, Hastings and Surrounding Area* all at 1:50,000
Accommodation:	Blackboys - Youth Hostel
	Elsewhere - b&b in Buxted (2½ miles north-west of Blackboys)
	b&b in East Hoathly (3 miles south of Blackboys)

From Forest Row the Vanguard Way quickly climbs onto Ashdown Forest, which it then spends some time in crossing. There are broad panoramas to enjoy up here, both to north and south. In some places it is possible on a clear day to see both the North Downs and the South Downs, but the Forest also has its little valleys too, with isolated cottages and small hamlets.

South of Ashdown Forest the route goes once more through a landscape of farmland; rolling meadows with sheep grazing, and more woodlands and among clusters of houses set in a land of welcome. One of the highlights is the countryside around the tiny village of High Hurstwood; but it's perhaps a little invidious to select one corner out of many enchanting corners. This is a stretch to bring pleasure with its continued variety.

The Vanguard Way reached Forest Row beside the Foresters Arms pub. Here turn left and go along the B2110 road for about 300 yards as far as a public telephone kiosk. Cross the road and take the footpath which leads half-left across a green to a road. Continue along the path that goes between the fences of several gardens and brings you to a residential road. Turn right for 200 yards, and near the brow of the hill, just before the road curves to the right, cross over and take the rough track that climbs up to the edge of a golf course. This is the start of Ashdown Forest.(1)

Turn left on a metalled road, and left again where it forks. Follow this narrow road across the golf course winding downhill until it comes to a house on the right, name of Shalesbrook. From here continue directly ahead on a rough track. About 100 yards further on there's another house on the right; Shaleshurst. Choose the left fork, cross a stream by a footbridge and soon after head right on a surfaced track for 40 yards. A rough track now leads left heading between woods and a golf course fairway. *Whilst crossing the golf course, take care, especially*

Ashdown Forest half an hour out of Forest Row

near fairways. You pass a tee on the right and the track (a bridle path) crosses a fairway with another tee, this time to the left. Follow the bridle path through the woods, keeping a fence to the left. It crosses a metalled track, then goes over a forded stream.

When the main track heads off to the right, with a tee on the left, go straight ahead on a rough trail leading uphill, going between woods and a fairway. Continue along the trail, passing on the left a house and a garage. A little over 100 yards further on bear right where the path forks to the left. Shortly after, views open to show the spire of Coleman's Hatch(2) church off to the left, standing out among trees.

Continue along the track. After reaching another tee the way crosses a small stream then heads uphill, veering to the right and leaving the golf course. Keep along the track until the top of the rise where another track heads off to the left. At this point there are splendid views to the north. One hundred yards along this track go right to reach the road. (Grid ref: 448330)

Cross this narrow road to a track opposite and follow this as it leads right and goes along two sides of a bowling green. Now cross a metalled lane and head half-right past a cricket pitch to its far side.

'The Splash' at Newbridge, Ashdown Forest

Here the track forks. Turn left, then after 50 yards bear right on an obvious track. Turn left at the next junction of routes, and after 100 yards reach a narrow metalled lane. Continue straight ahead on this lane until it brings you to a minor road. Turn right and walk along this road for about a quarter of a mile until you reach a row of cottages on the right-hand side of the road at Newbridge, almost opposite a ford known as 'The Splash'. Cross the road and take the little footbridge beside the ford, and 60 yards along the lane bear half-right on a vague grassy trail that climbs uphill between a hedge on the left and woodland to the right. There's a house off to the left. Where the hedge branches off leftwards the trail veers to the right. About 300 yards beyond this you come to a junction of tracks. Turn left and at the following junction go right and keep on the same path heading uphill. This eventually brings you to a superb viewpoint, some 80 yards to the west of a stand of pines known as Gills Lap Clump.

Gills Lap Clump is one of the highest parts of Ashdown Forest and around it there lies a strange rolling heathland, charred here and there by the occasional summer fires that threaten to destroy it. The sun was full upon me as I topped the rise, and I shrugged off the rucksack and slumped in the heather to enjoy the views. They were certainly vast, especially to the north where the heath sloped away to trees, while far off the deep stretch of the Weald gulped a sultry blue light and the distant hills shimmered through a veil of evaporation.

Continue along the track, veering right to reach a car park where ice creams are often available from a van. Cross the rough car park and come to a road junction. Go over the main road to a track and follow this straight ahead for 100 yards. Now bear right on another track that follows the direction of the road for a little over half a mile towards a 'spinney' of lofty radio masts. Along this track crosses the route of the Wealdway. Shortly after, the track comes to the road at another rough car park. Continue ahead along the edge of the road for about 100 yards to reach a junction with the B2188. (Grid ref: 473302) Opposite there's another car park with seats and picnic tables and, for much of the year, an ice cream van. Beyond this car park an attractive stand of pines, known as King's Standing Clump,(3) is circled by paths. Go round it to the right, then turn left on a track that leads in 100 yards to a crosstrack. Continue straight ahead, following the crest of a broad 'ridge' for almost half a mile. There are wide views to enjoy as you wander along this ridge, especially off to the hint of the South Downs forming a distant horizon.

The ridge runs out with a steep slope of hill falling away before you. Several paths converge here and you must bear half-right on a path that follows the contour of the hill for a brief stretch before heading downhill towards a stream and a boggy section. *This meagre stream oozing from the hillside is one of the sources of the Medway, that fine river of Kent that has seen so much of England's history.*

The track bears left, crosses another stream 100 yards later on, then continues straight ahead over a wooden bridge and uphill for a little under half a mile. Near the top of the slope there's a little wood on the right. Then the route passes a garden and a house on the right, and brings you to the A26 Tunbridge Wells to Lewes road. This marks the end of the crossing of Ashdown Forest.

Turn left on the road and walk towards the Crow and Gate pub about 250 yards away on the edge of Poundgate. Just before the pub, cross the road and go through a wooden gate near a telephone kiosk. Cross the field towards a house and pass through a second gate. A concrete track leads between houses, then go through a metal gate after about 30 yards. Views here show the South Downs in the distance. Turn sharp right across the field, then through another

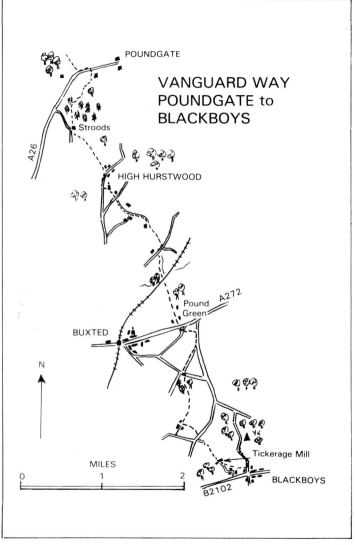

POUNDGATE

VANGUARD WAY
POUNDGATE to
BLACKBOYS

Stroods

A26

HIGH HURSTWOOD

Pound
Green   A272

BUXTED

N

MILES

Tickerage Mill

BLACKBOYS

0   1   2

B2102

Delightful country near High Hurstwood on the Vanguard Way

metal gate after 70 yards. Pass along the right-hand edge of the field, then left on a sunken track beside a hedge. By way of a metal gate you now enter the wood ahead. After some 30 yards turn right on a vague path, close to the side of the wood. The path eventually brings you to a stile that leads out to a field. Bear left along the edge of this field and at the end, find a stile beside a field gate and go into the woods once more. Continue straight ahead through the woods on a clear track, ignoring all side turnings, until you come to a cottage on the right. Leave the wood by way of a stile and follow along the right-hand boundary of the field for 100 yards. This leads to houses at Stroods Farm. The path goes ahead between holly bushes, through a garden and beside the houses to reach a metalled farm road.

One of the features of walking in a rural landscape in England is this occasional 'trespass' through farmyards or across the lawns of private houses. It is a right that goes back a long way, but the walker must never forget that this right is also a privilege that should not be put in jeopardy. On the Vanguard Way there are several instances where the route intrudes on the property of others, right beside the homes of country dwellers. Please respect the privacy of those whose gardens you tread.

Turn right on the farm road, and a few yards farther on make a sharp left. Twenty yards later, at Wiltshiers, head along the right fork on a rough track, then a short distance along this take the left-hand of two metal gates. Bear half-left diagonally across the field, ignoring the stile seen halfway along the fence, and cross a stile by a gate in the far left-hand corner. Continue into the next field, then follow the fence leading downhill to a stile on the right with a finger post pointing to High Hurstwood.

A few yards above this stile the bank beyond the fence was massed with bluebells, while the little spinney threw a welcome shade. I sat there in the grass with a cuckoo hiccuping in the trees and a pair of larks singing their arias especially for me. A breeze tempered the afternoon's heat, and I was aware of my good fortune in being there at that moment in time, in a landscape of green unspoilt by anything that could be considered out of place, with the peace of the day unbroken by sounds of traffic or radios, and the sweet taste of warm grass on my tongue. All round the world was green; woods, meadows, the fields of young corn. It was the sort of English countryside that brings deep satisfaction to those who wander through it. It's not high or rugged or carved by swirling rivers; just a gentle land of greenery, soft and mature with the houses and church of High Hurstwood showing as toys among the trees beyond the sloping hill. That way led my path.

Cross the stile and go downhill with those magnificent views drawing you on, with the field fence on your left. In the far corner of the field cross another stile and continue down between fences to a bridge. Over the bridge the path now climbs steeply to a track beside some houses. Follow this track to reach the road. This is the little village of High Hurstwood. (Grid ref: 494267)

Turn right along the road for 200 yards, then head left on a drive leading to Holy Trinity church. Just before reaching this church you'll find a kissing gate on the right. Go through into a field and aim towards two large oak trees. Behind them go through another kissing gate and follow the path as it leads between hedges and comes out to a lawn beside a house. Cross the drive here and go through a narrow kissing gate, up a field to yet another kissing gate which brings you to a road.

Cross the road and take the track ahead. Turn left at the next road, some way after the track has become surfaced. The road deteriorates to a rough track again after passing some houses. The track curves to the right, and 50 yards beyond this go straight ahead through a metal gate onto a grass track between hedges at Holderns Farm. Cross a stile and continue ahead, over a footbridge in a little 'valley' by some trees. Now go straight ahead over a field to its far corner, to pass through a metal gate. Go diagonally half-left up the field to the corner some 50 yards left of a barn, and go through a gate onto the road beyond.

Turn right on the road for about 100 yards, then go left across a stile beside a metal gate and into a field. Head down towards the wood with a pleasant stream, cross a set of wooden bars and a stile and follow along the left-hand edge of the next field as far as the end of the wood. Now continue over the field, cross a footbridge and another stile and, continuing along the path, go straight ahead through woods and under a railway arch. Over the next stile turn right on a track going through trees to a field. Straight ahead over the field, make for the right-hand corner of a wood and find a stile beside a wooden gate. With woods on your left continue uphill on a path. This becomes a track which leads to the A272 road. (Grid ref: 508237)

Note: *For those requiring either b&b accommodation or British Rail transport to East Croydon, London or Uckfield, turn right here and follow the road for about ¾ mile into Buxted.*

Cross the road and turn left, then take the turning on the right signposted to Potters Green. Almost at once leave the road and take the drive heading left to Pound Cottage. Where the drive curves to the right, leave it and go ahead towards the entrance to a field. Here follow the footpath which runs to the left of a wire fence and leads to another road. Turn right and follow this road for about ¾ mile to a crossroads. Do not be tempted to take the first turning on the left which is signposted to Blackboys.

Note: *On reaching the crossroads (Grid ref: 509227) you have a choice to make. Those planning to stay overnight at Blackboys Youth Hostel may shorten their journey by a road walk of a little over a mile - details in Alternative Route 1 below. Or one could continue the route of the Vanguard Way for a further two miles or so, and then turn back on a road for just over half a mile - Alternative Route 2. The second option is the more attractive.*

Alternative Route 1:

Turn left at the crossroads and follow the road with fine views over the fields to the right, as far as another junction. Here turn right. The road climbs a little and comes to a fork. Turn left and follow this

Blackboys Youth Hostel - suitable overnight accommodation on both routes

minor road for about a quarter of a mile and take the first turning on the right. This loses height with woods on either side. About 400 yards along this road you come to Blackboys Youth Hostel set back in the woods on the left.

Blackboys Youth Hostel: *A set of wooden hutments originally built to house refugees from the Spanish Civil War, it stands in pleasant woodlands. Simple grade, it has 40 beds in dormitories. Hot showers, self-catering facilities, small store. No meals provided. Camping permissible in the gounds. See the current YHA Guide for up-to-date information on opening dates and times, and also for present charges. Telephone: Framfield (082582) 607.*

Vanguard Way Continuation (Avoiding Alternative 1):

Turn left along the road, and 50 yards later turn right on a path heading through trees. This is a very pleasant stretch, especially in spring with a dazzle of bluebells. Downhill the path bears leftwards. It takes you to a gate and farm buildings which you pass on your left.

Cross wooden bars and a fence and follow along the right-hand edge of a field for 50 yards, then follow the path directly ahead among trees running between fields. This stretch can be a little tangled. Cross a stream by way of a footbridge, and once the stream curves off to the left, cross to the corner of the field on your left. Turn right along its edge, but when it veers to the right go straight ahead towards a small orchard. Bear left through a metal gate to the left of a corrugated iron barn. Immediately after, turn left on a track and go through a gate, continuing ahead towards trees and the corner of a hedge. Go to the left of the hedge and follow the track as far as a road.

Turn right on the road and 150 yards farther on go left through a gate and onto a track. In another 150 yards go straight ahead with a wood on your right, and downhill go through a gate and over a field to a track which runs between a lake on the left and houses on the right. This is Tickerage Mill, and here the Vanguard Way crosses the route of the Wealdway once more.

Both routes pass the lake and the rather elegant house on the left, to reach a driveway. Go up this for about 80 yards. You'll find a metal gate on your left. Here the Vanguard Way departs again from the Wealdway. Go through the gate and rise among trees to follow the right-hand boundary of the field. Pass through a gap and cross the next field bearing half-right on a vague path towards a line of trees. Pass to the right of these going uphill to reach a stile beside a gate. Over this follow the path to a lane. Turn left, and 30 yards later go right on a track entering an area of allotments. Take the footpath left to a road.

Alternative Route 2:

At this road head left for Blackboys Youth Hostel. Follow the road for a little over half a mile. The hostel is found in the woods set back on the right.

Vanguard Way Continuation (Avoiding Youth Hostel):

Turn right on the road to reach the B2102 at a crossroads. (Grid ref: 522207) Cross straight over and follow down the road opposite to reach the Blackboys Inn standing on the right beside the B2192.

Blackboys is a small village whose name is supposedly derived from the charcoal burners of a previous age; ie. 'black boys'. It boasts a couple of pubs, a post office and general stores, and while much of the village is fairly modern, the Blackboys Inn was built as a farmhouse in 1389, and converted as an Inn early in the 18th century. All around lies a pleasant agricultural landscape, with the Downs little more than a faint hint in the distance.

Things Seen On The Way:

1. *Ashdown Forest* covers an area of more than 6,000 acres; all that remains of the once vast Forest of Anderida. Nowadays the Forest consists of a high open heathland, with stands of pine here and there. The Saxons were responsible for a considerable amount of forest clearance, and by the time the Normans arrived the surrounding area was mostly settled, leaving only the high ground of today's Forest without any real habitation.

The Forest is administered by a Board of Conservators who have, since 1885, had the express purpose of exercising jurisdiction over all matters concerning it. Apart from observing the Country Code, the by-laws of Ashdown Forest have one item which may effect Vanguard Way wanderers, and that concerns camping or bivouacking on the Forest, both of which are forbidden.

2. *Coleman's Hatch* is by-passed on our route, but the church of Holy Trinity is seen from parts of Ashdown Forest. The name Coleman's Hatch comes from the landowner who erected a Forest gate (or Hatch) here; certainly before 1495.

3. *King's Standing Clump*. This lovely stand of pines is traditionally the place where Edward II hid whilst hunting deer. He built a palace nearby and used Ashdown Forest as a royal hunting ground. This was in the 14th century, and the palace has long since disappeared.

Public Transport On Section 3:

Forest Row details are given at the end of Section 2.
Buxted has a British Rail station on the line serving Edenbridge Town, East Croydon and London; and Uckfield in the opposite direction. No services on Sundays.
Blackboys has a Southdown bus service on the Uckfield to Eastbourne route. Also, rarely, to Brighton and Canterbury.

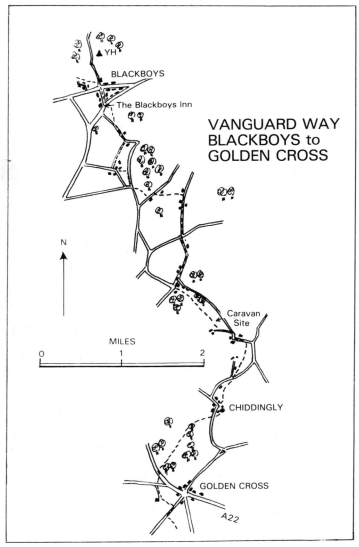

VANGUARD WAY
BLACKBOYS to
GOLDEN CROSS

SECTION 4: BLACKBOYS TO ALFRISTON

Distance:	15 miles
Map:	O.S. Landranger series; Sheet 199 *Eastbourne,* *Hastings and Surrounding Area* 1:50,000
Accommodation:	Alfriston - Hotels, Youth Hostel, b&b

This stage has an air of expectation about it as the Downs gradually impose on the south bound walker, and you know that the sea is not far off. There are some interesting corners to explore, some very pleasant countryside to wander through. But this is the hardest stage of the whole walk, for some of the paths are a little difficult to find in places. Let this not deter you, however, for there's much to inspire your day - and there's no better way of ensuring that footpaths become clearer than that of regular use by walkers.

The route goes through meadows and woodlands, often with fine views, to reach the little village of Chiddingly with its lovely 13th century church. Then it works its way southward into a more open series of landscapes under huge skies, drawing closer to the gap in the Downs cut by the Cuckmere River. The Vanguard Way makes a beeline for Berwick Station on the Eastbourne to Lewes line, then across fields to Berwick village; a charming spot on the home straight to Alfriston - one of the most frequented villages in all Sussex.

From the Blackboys Inn cross the B2192 and enter a field by way of a stile in the hedge. Cut straight over the field down to a stile by a willow tree. Cross this and go along the left-hand side of the next field to reach a road. Here turn left. In about 500 yards the road curves to the left; leave it here and turn right on a little track through a wooden gate beside the entrance to Bushmere. The track deteriorates to a narrow path, sometimes a little tangled, and brings you to another road. Turn left. After a short while the road bends to the right by some houses. Instead of following it, go straight ahead on a path to the left of a white gate, cross a stile and go along the right-hand edge of the field to a road. Turn right on this until you come to the first road junction. Here turn left through a gate and head diagonally half-right across the large field aiming towards the corner of a wood. Before reaching it, however, bear right again and follow along the edge of the wood to reach a road. (Grid ref: 530184)

Turn left and wander along the road for about 100 yards towards a bungalow with a landscaped garden. Turn right just before this on a track and continue straight ahead over the field. Enter a second field through a gap and turn left, following the hedge to a stile in the corner. Cross this and turn right, but after 60 yards head half-left downhill to a gateway and a bridge among trees. Cross this bridge and walk uphill through a field making towards the top right-hand corner, then cross an awkward stile by a gate and come onto another road.

Once on the road turn right and follow it for a little over half a mile and come to a road junction. Turn right and then almost immediately go left and face a further half mile or so of road walking. You will come to a road branching off to the left; ignore this but continue for another 100 yards where you reach another junction. (The road on the right is signposted to East Hoathly - where the Wealdway passes through.) Leave the road and go left through a gate seen to the left of Graywood House, and head along a track by the side of the house. Just before reaching a shed, find a footpath bearing left through trees. This path crosses a driveway and enters a private garden, going straight ahead through an archway of roses. (A delight at any time of the year, but especially so when the roses are in bloom.)

The path continues ahead through woods until you come to a stile. Go across a track and over another stile. Keep to the left-hand field boundary as far as a gate at the end of the field. There are some welcome views of the South Downs off to the right. Go through a gate, but then cross to the left into a field used as a caravan site. Follow the hedge now on your right to the end of this field, then pass back to the right of the hedge as before; turn left to maintain the same direction. After about 20 yards the path crosses back to the left-hand field through a gate, but goes forward again, still in the same direction. At the first corner of the field boundary, which heads to the right, cross the field to find a gate in the right-hand corner. This in turn brings you to a driveway. Turn left, but on reaching a road turn right. You come to Chiswells Farm, and some 200 yards beyond it, turn right over a stile in the hedge. There is a stone marker on the ground. (Grid ref: 549155)

I sat in the field with my back to the stile gazing south across the meadows towards the spire of Chiddingly church. Beyond that folded the Downs. It was a quiet stretch of country; peaceful in the mid-morning hum of late spring, and as I sat there enjoying a moment's relaxation, I became aware of rabbits playing nearby, quite oblivious of my presence. When I stood up to continue the walk, a cock pheasant with a yard-long tail burst out of the grass almost at my feet and set my heart pounding with shock. It flew low over the field and landed right on my path, so I had to disturb him yet again.

Cross the field to the left corner of a fence, then continue with the fence on your right. This is replaced by a hedge. Keep along the right-hand side of more fields often linked with awkward stiles. On reaching a road turn right. Forty yards on, turn left through a kissing gate and head straight across the field to a stile. It may be a little boggy here. Go along the right side of the following field to a stile, then uphill on the left-hand side of the next field as far as a gate. Pass through this and cross the field towards a stile, beyond which you wander along the left-hand boundary of this field, aiming towards the church. Over another stile and along a stretch of hedge-bound footpath, you come into the little village of Chiddingly.(1) Here, once more, the Wealdway and Vanguard Way cross tracks.

Turn left towards the church, passing in front of the Post Office Stores. (The Six Bells pub is off to the right.) Enter the churchyard and take the pathway going to the right. This leads through to a stile; beyond is a playing field and cricket pitch.

I went inside the church at noon, into the welcome cool and sat for a few minutes listening to the silence of seven hundred years. The walls with their monuments had a history to speak. Saints in stained glass shredded the light and the clock overhead marked the passage of time. Through the centuries, thousands had come here to worship and to seek the comfort of fellowship. Hundreds had marked the most important events of their lives here; infant baptism, marriage, and finally their passage from this earth. Alone, I knew a profound sense of well-being there, and witnessed a gratitude for the day. I went on my way refreshed.

Cross out of the churchyard and into the playing field. Cross this with the pavilion to your right, and reach a gate which leads out to a road. Cross the road half-left to another gate into a field. Head diagonally half-left over this field, making for a hedge corner and towards a wood. Pass through a gate and maintain the same direction to locate a stile leading into the wood. Follow the path through to another stile. Now turn left along the edge of the field to find yet another stile by a pond. A footbridge leads into a small plantation and a large field beyond. After about 50 yards head into the field, half-right, making for a point roughly a little to the right of a centre between two woods. As you top the slight rise in the field, make for a stile which you will find more or less halfway along the hedge on the field boundary.

Over the stile and into the next field, head a little leftwards to reach a stile by some oak trees. A plank bridge takes you over a ditch, then

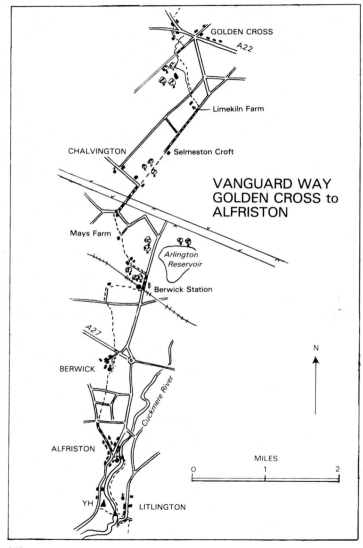

GOLDEN CROSS

A22

Limekiln Farm

CHALVINGTON

Selmeston Croft

VANGUARD WAY
GOLDEN CROSS to
ALFRISTON

Mays Farm

Arlington
Reservoir

Berwick Station

A27

N

BERWICK

Cuckmere River

ALFRISTON

MILES

0   1   2

YH

LITLINGTON

Limekiln Farm on the Vanguard Way

you must aim directly ahead over this field to a gate leading into the next field. Here bear a little to the right towards an angle bend in the woods. There you will find a stile which leads into the woods. Another stile gives access to a small field and out onto the busy A22 road. (Grid ref: 532129)

Cross the road and turn left to walk towards The Wattle teashop. Just before you reach this, however, turn right and fight your way down an overgrown path between hedges. (If this is no longer overgrown, be thankful; if it is, curse along with me!) Cross over the fence and keep to the right-hand side of the field to reach the B2124. Cross this road and take the track ahead. Where it forks, go through the gateway straight ahead, signposted to Brickfields Farm. In the yard among buildings take the track going off to the left and pass through a metal gate. Leave the track in front of a barn and go over a stile into the next field, going straight over this to reach another road through a gate. Here turn right and follow the road for about 200 yards until you reach some white railings on either side of the road. Now go left over a difficult stile and bear half-right towards a hedge. Follow along this hedge to find a gate in the top right corner of the field. Cross the following field to a hedge, and then go through a gap, over a stile and a ditch and then wander along the right-hand boundary of the next three fields. So come to another road. Turn right and walk along this for about 70 yards, then go left along a drive through a white gate leading to Limekiln Farm.(2)

The drive gives the Vanguard Way walker a most enjoyable stroll beside a stream that almost makes a moat along the northern edge of Limekiln Farm; a beautiful timbered building with an oast - without a cowl - set beside it. Ducks were contenting themselves in the stream as I walked past, and the banks were a mass of flowers. The whole scene was quite delightful.

As the drive bends to the right, continue straight ahead to find a gate leading to a footpath through the next field. Another gate to the left of a house brings you to a lane. Turn right and follow along this for the next mile or so. It's a quiet lane whose dye-straight alignment gives a hint to its Roman origins. (See the note on Limekiln Farm at the end of this Section.)

On arriving at Selmeston Croft, a house on the left with views off to the Downs, the metalled lane comes to an end. In its place there stretches a grassy track. Continue straight ahead along this. Unfortunately, this track soon deteriorates into a muddy and sometimes waterlogged mire among trees. It is probably the worst piece of the whole route, but happily, although the track is almost ¾ mile long, the worst of it affects only a comparatively short stretch. Eventually, and with some relief, you come onto another quiet road a little under half a mile south-east of the hamlet of Chalvington. (Grid ref: 525091)

Go straight ahead along this road until you come to a junction. Turn right, go just beyond some buildings on the left, then take the stile on your left, with more fine views of the Downs. Skirt the field by its left-hand boundary to reach a stile in the first corner. Cross over and in the next field make towards the building of Mays Farm to the right. Go through a gap in the hedge and use a plank footbridge to cross a ditch, then over a stile. Now cross the field going uphill to find a gate left of the farm buildings. Walk through the farmyard and cross the approach road to the left of more buildings. Go round a pond and along the back of the buildings. You'll see a metal gate on your left, not far from the end of the flint wall leading to the rather impressive house. Go through the gate to enter the large open field.

In the absence of a clear path on the ground, head towards a metal barn seen behind some trees. You will come to a stile and a bridge that take you directly into another field. Now go towards the house seen to the left of the barn. The path takes you over another stile and through the garden of the house; between the house itself and a picturesque pond. Once across this take the drive to its end where it meets a road, with Arlington Reservoir a short distance away. Turn right and walk along the road to Berwick Station. (Trains from here go to Eastbourne, Lewes and Brighton.)

An attractive corner of Berwick village on the Vanguard Way

Cross the railway line and turn right immediately before a large warehouse-type building just beyond the level crossing. Passing between a shed and a fence, take the track up a slope to a gate leading into a large field. Keep to the boundary on the right for some sixty yards, then branch away diagonally half-left across the field to locate a pair of gates that grant access to the next field. With the hedge on your right go along the headland of this field, eventually to pass in front of Stonery Farm with its commanding view out to the south. Shortly after, bear left on the farm track and wander down this to the road. Turn left along the road for about 50 yards and find a gate in the hedge on your right. Cross the road, go through the gate and head straight down across the field to a line of trees where you will find a stile and a plank bridge over a stream.

Note: *This bridge was in an extremely dangerous condition in 1986, and if it has not been improved, great care should be exercised when crossing. On the other side there may be some difficulty in route finding, due to changes in the layout of fields and the felling of some trees. You are aiming*

*for the village of Berwick, which is almost due south of the point at which
you entered the field from the road. But first, having crossed the stream, you
must go a little south of south-east. The following route description
appertains to conditions in late spring 1986.*

Turn left and follow along the edge of the field until you reach a
culvert. Cross this and turn right, soon to reach a stile. Cross the stile
and head a little left across this field - you will see Berwick church
almost directly ahead. At the bottom of the field go through a gate and
into the next field. Cut straight across, making towards a line of elect-
ricity poles that meet in a hedge corner. There you will find another
stile which leads into another field. Walk along this, keeping to its
right-hand edge. Where the field finishes cross a stream by way of a
stile and plank footbridge, and bear left across this last field to a metal
gate that brings you onto the hectic A27 Eastbourne to Lewes road.
(Grid ref: 520054)

Turn left and wander along the road for about 30 yards, then cross
with great care to a quiet road that leads into Berwick village; an
attractive corner with many pleasing faces. Turn left opposite the
Cricketers Arms on a gravel drive that leads round a pond, and pass in
front of a lovely old barn, then left along the side of the barn to a stile.
Go between some fine large chestnut trees, and at the top of the field
keep left of the 12th century church of St. Michael and All Angels(3)
to cross a stile onto a track leading past the church. The track curves
right behind the church, but the Vanguard Way goes straight ahead
on an obvious path, and becomes a veritable switchback as it heads
across the hills over a series of stiles in a straight line, before coming
into a lane which runs down into Alfriston. It's a lovely final walk,
with an attractive village at the end of it.

Note: *For those planning to stay overnight at Alfriston Youth Hostel, see
the opening paragraph of Section 5 which follows.*

*Alfriston is something of a show-piece village and is invariably crowded
with day trippers. Its streets are lined with interesting and picturesque
buildings, many of them with flint walls, so typical of the Downs. Among
the most notable are the Clergy House, a thatched, half-timbered priest's
house dating from the 14th century and the first building acquired by the
National Trust (for £10!) in 1896; the George Inn, a one-time smugglers'
haunt, built in 1397; the Star Inn, a 15th century half-timbered building
bearing a carved lion that had once been the figurehead of a Dutch ship
which foundered in Cuckmere Haven; and of course, the church of St.And-*

The lovely 14th century George Inn, Alfriston on the Vanguard Way

rew, a 14th century flint building sometimes referred to as the Cathedral of
the Downs on account of its size. The village, sitting above the winding
Cuckmere River, with the Downs on either side, offers one of the highlights
of the journey from suburbs to the sea.

Things Seen On The Way:

1. *Chiddingly* is one of those pleasant discoveries that gives a bonus to
the walker's day. There's not much of it, to be true. A few houses and
farms - one of which, Place Farm on the route of the Wealdway, is a
curious mass of bricks on the site of an Elizabethan mansion - the Six
Bells pub, a Post Office Stores and a lovely church with a stone spire.
The church is about 700 years old; the tower and spire were added in
the fifteenth century. This spire is one of the only three such stone
spires in all of Sussex; it rises to almost 130 feet and is completely
hollow with walls only a foot thick. In 1897 it was damaged by lightning, after which a massive chain was fixed around the tower. It
houses six bells - hence the name of the nearby pub - the oldest of

which is said to be 350 years old. Among the memorials in the church is a rather busy one to the Jefferay family of Place Farm.

2. *Limekiln Farm*, south-west of Lower Dicker, is a beautiful timbered building set in delightful grounds. The Vanguard Way leads in front of it alongside a stream that makes an attractive moat. It is interesting to learn that more than 1600 years ago the Romans managed a substantial agricultural estate around here. The dead-straight line of several roads and tracks that cross this region, give evidence of their origin.

3. *Berwick Church*, dedicated to St. Michael and All Angels, is worth a visit. It occupies a splendid hilltop site where it has stood for eight centuries. The interior has some interesting contrasting styles, including an ancient font and a collection of murals painted during the last war by local artists. Outside, the churchyard has a Saxon burial mound.

Public Transport On Section 4:

Blackboys details are given at the end of Section 3.

Golden Cross (south of Chiddingly) has Southdown bus services to Hailsham, Eastbourne, Uckfield and East Grinstead.

Berwick Station is on the Eastbourne, Lewes and Brighton railway line. An hourly service.

Berwick has S.D. buses to Lewes, Polegate and Eastbourne.

Alfriston is served by S.D. buses running to Seaford, Polegate and Eastbourne.

SECTION 5: ALFRISTON TO SEAFORD HEAD

Distance:	6 miles
Map:	O.S. Landranger series; Sheet 199 *Eastbourne, Hastings and Surrounding Area* 1:50,000
Accommodation:	Seaford - Hotels and b&b

This final stage offers an easy morning's walk along the South Downs, sharing in places the route of the South Downs Way. It's a lovely walk, filled with a variety of interesting scenes. It goes through the villages of Littlington and Westdean, traverses the shady Friston Forest and comes out to a fine view of the winding ox-bows of the Cuckmere River. The route then drops down to the river, crosses it at Exceat Bridge, and follows the right bank as far as its meeting with the sea at Cuckmere Haven where the Seven Sisters arch their way in white cliff and green Down towards Beachy Head. From Cuckmere Haven the Vanguard Way turns its back on the Seven Sisters to climb the grassy cliff-top path to Seaford Head, journey's end and a world away from East Croydon where it began.

A short downhill stroll leads from Seaford Head into the town of Seaford with its hotels, guest houses and cafés. The homebound traveller then has a choice of either bus to Brighton or Eastbourne (with their own rail connections), or by British Rail to Lewes (for London) and Brighton. Or, perhaps better still, extend the walk with an addition of four hours or so along the cliffs to Eastbourne before facing the journey home.

From the village square at Alfriston go along the main street southward to pass The George Inn. About 25 yards beyond this, turn left along an alley on a footpath. Keep on the left-hand path where it forks. This takes you to the left of the church and drops down to the river. Cross the Cuckmere by way of the wooden bridge, then immediately turn right over a stile and follow the riverside footpath for the next mile. A pleasant and easy stroll, with the village of Littlington coming into view ahead at the foot of the Downs.

Note: *On reaching the next bridge, those planning to stay overnight at Alfriston Youth Hostel must leave the Vanguard Way on Alternative Route 1 below.*

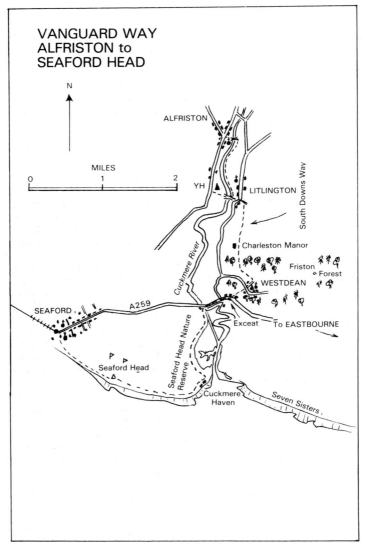

VANGUARD WAY
ALFRISTON to
SEAFORD HEAD

N

MILES

0   1   2

ALFRISTON

YH   LITLINGTON

South Downs Way

Cuckmere River

Charleston Manor

Friston
Forest

WESTDEAN

SEAFORD   A259

Exceat   To EASTBOURNE

Seaford Head Nature Reserve

Seaford Head

Cuckmere
Haven   Seven Sisters

Alternative Route 1:

Cross the bridge over the river and follow the path as it climbs uphill to reach a road. The building immediately on the right is Frog Firle, the Youth Hostel.

Alfriston Youth Hostel: A large flint built house dating partially from 1530, with lovely views over the Cuckmere's valley. Superior grade, it has beds for 65 in dormitories. Hot showers, meals provided, self-cookers' kitchen, small store and drying facilities. Telephone: Alfriston (0323) 870423. See the current YHA Guide for up-to-date information on opening dates and times, and also for present charges.

Vanguard Way Continuation (Avoiding Youth Hostel):

At the bridge turn left and follow the path into Littlington village, which has some pretty corners. Turn right on the road and shortly after, you pass The Plough and Harrow pub. After this cross the road and turn left into a lane. A few yards along this lane you will find a kissing gate on your right, with a stone marking the South Downs Way. Go through the gate and follow the path uphill, making for a stile in the top left-hand corner of the field. For the next mile and a half the Vanguard Way will be following the South Downs Way(1) and enjoying the comfort of its waymarking, only to leave it at Exceat.

Cross the stile and continue ahead on the left-hand side of the next field with views off to the right across the valley to a white horse seen carved in chalk on the distant Downs. After this field cross two more stiles and go along the right-hand side of the next. Another stile, then the path drops downhill towards woodlands, on the edge of which sits Charleston Manor.(2)

At the foot of the slope cross a stile and turn left. Follow the path which becomes an enclosed one, then head to the right and climb a series of steps into the large, mainly broad leaved Friston Forest.(3) At the top of the steep incline there's another stile. Continue ahead on a broad track for some distance, following the South Downs Way acorn signs all the way to Westdean.(4) On reaching a road, wander along it to the bottom of the hill where you come to a junction next to a lovely old house. The road which crosses leads through the village. Opposite is a most delightful spot; a pond, alive with ducks, at the foot of another section of Friston Forest.

Cross the road to a track left of the pond. There are houses on your left, and beside the track a Forestry Commission notice board. Go

*The Vanguard Way shares the route of the South Downs Way
to climb into Friston Forest near Charleston Manor*

ahead to find another set of steps - more than two hundred of them! -
that take you once more up into Friston Forest. The footpath
continues directly ahead through the forest, eventually to emerge at a
low wall with a built-in stone stile.

152

Suddenly the views opened out and there was space again. Not just space but a flooding of light; the Downs and the sky, and off to the left the gleam of water and the smell of the sea. There was a marvellous panorama that called for a rest, so I sat below the wall and simply gazed with pleasure. Across the valley the Downs folded neatly to the sea; green and smooth they were, wrinkle free yet soft. But steeply below the Cuckmere had wound itself through green water meadows in search of an outlet to the salt water haven. How this river had niggled for thousands of years at the chalk to free itself from the hold of the land! Now it looked tired from its ageless industry, and could relax with the knowledge that the sea would draw it on. Below me it glinted in the morning sunlight; a lovely view that had been worth the journey, yet acceptance that this journey was almost at an end made me a little reluctant, like the Cuckmere itself, to uncurl myself and find that haven.

Cross the stile and descend the grassy slopes to the foot of the hill where another stile leads between buildings onto the traffic mad A259 Seaford to Eastbourne road. This is Exceat, a one-time settlement that flourished until the Black Death virtually wiped it off the map in the 15th century. Turning right on this road you come shortly to the Seven Sisters Country Park Centre on your right. Cross the road and continue along to the right. The Cuckmere here looks delightful on your left. You will come to a bridge taking traffic over the river. On the other side is The Golden Galleon. Cross the bridge and enter the car park to find a stile leading onto a track. Follow this track for nearly a quarter of a mile, then over a stile to enter Seaford Head Nature Reserve.(5)

Continue ahead along the path which remains a short distance from the right bank of the river, until it divides shortly before reaching some exposed houses on the cliff edge at Cuckmere Haven.(6) Take the left fork to the stony beach for a view along the face of the Seven Sisters cliffs, then turn away to the right on a path which goes beside the houses. Now fork leftwards on a grassy cliff path that leads in a little over a mile to an airy golf course and the concrete trig point atop Seaford Head. This is the official end of the Vanguard Way; a lofty cliff with a view of the sea.

It has taken 62 miles to reach this belvedere from the scurrying commuters and towering office blocks of Croydon, and it is my hope that, as I did, you will find it sufficient reward for having completed it. The Vanguard Way may be over in the physical sense, but hopefully you will take with you many pleasant memories to reflect upon in the months and years ahead.

The Cuckmere at Exceat - seen from the Vanguard Way

From Seaford Head you have a choice to make for the homeward journey. You can drop down on the cliff path to Seaford, which is seen below, and there catch a train or bus back home. Or, alternatively, if you have time and energy left, add four or five hours more walking to your day and stride over the Seven Sisters to Birling Gap, then up and over Beachy Head before dropping down into Eastbourne where there are train and bus services homeward. In order to reach the Seven Sisters entails a retracing of the Vanguard Way as far as Exceat Bridge, then follow the Cuckmere towards Cuckmere Haven once more, but this time on its left bank. A path then leads up onto the first of the Seven Sisters. It's a magnificent walk, and is thoroughly recommended.

Things Seen On The Way:

1. *The South Downs Way* is one of the most popular of all Britain's long distance walks. It stretches for 80 miles between Eastbourne and Buriton, although there are plans to extend it beyond there.

The Seven Sisters seen from the path up to Seaford Head

2. *Charleston Manor,* on the edge of Friston Forest, is an historic and lovely building that goes back to the 11th century, and is mentioned in the Domesday Book. In the grounds stands a large barn dating from the 15th century, and fine stables two hundred years old. Both the house and its delightful gardens are open to the public.

3. *Friston Forest,* leased by the Forestry Commission. This vast area covers almost 2,000 acres of largely broad leaved woodland, with some pine screening. There are several paths and rides through the Forest, including the South Downs Way, Forest Walk and Exceat Woodland Walk.

4. *Westdean.* Walkers are strongly advised to leave the Vanguard Way here for a few minutes to explore this delightful hamlet that has much of historic interest. It is said that Alfred the Great built a palace here in 850 AD, although there is no sign of one nowadays. Certainly the Priest's House, dating from the 11th century, is one of Britain's oldest homes still being occupied - and there's a 13th century Rectory too.

5. *Seaford Head Nature Reserve* reaches from a short distance down river below Exceat Bridge to Seaford Head, and covers an area of some 300 acres. Some of the plant species are rather uncommon - a leaflet obtainable from the Seven Sisters Country Park Centre tells you what to look for. But perhaps the most outstanding feature lies in the magnificent views from the clifftop which extend along the coast to the Seven Sisters in the east, and to the Isle of Wight in the west.

6. *Cuckmere Haven* is the estuary of the Cuckmere River; a lovely gap in the cliffs between the Seven Sisters and Seaford Head, the beach is stony and falls steeply into the sea. The Seven Sisters Country Park includes the eastern portion of it, and there are footpaths along the river on both banks from Exceat Bridge to the Haven, but no way from one to the other except at Exceat Bridge. Long ago, it is said, Alfred the Great had a shipyard here, and all around this corner of Sussex there are traditions appertaining to the reign of this Saxon king.

Cuckmere Haven was also very popular with smugglers, for the river made it possible to transport illicit cargoes inland to Exceat or Alfriston where they would either hide, or make good their escape across the Downs to Jevington or Wilmington.

Public Transport On Section 5:

Alfriston details are given at the end of Section 4.
Exceat is served by Southdown buses that run to Seaford, Brighton, Alfriston and Eastbourne.
Seaford has British Rail trains to Newhaven, Lewes and Brighton. S.D. buses go to Brighton, Alfriston and Eastbourne.
Eastbourne is conveniently serviced by British Rail and Southdown buses. The rail link is with Lewes, Hastings and Brighton; and a fast service to East Croydon and London. Southdown buses travel to various other coastal towns, as well as inland.

Useful Addresses

The Ramblers' Association
1-5 Wandsworth Road
London   SW8 2LJ

Youth Hostels Association
(England and Wales)
Trevelyan House
St. Albans
Herts   AL1 2DY

The Conservators of Ashdown
Forest
c/o The Village Hall
Forest Row
East Sussex

South-East England Tourist Board
1 Warwick Park
Tunbridge Wells
Kent   TN2 5BR

The Vanguards Rambling Club
c/o 109 Selsdon Park Road
South Croydon
Surrey   CR2 8JJ

In the heart of Forest Row

Public Transport Addresses

British Rail:
Southern Region
Essex House
College Road
Croydon   CR9 1NY

Bus Operators:
London Transport:
55 Broadway
London   SW1H 0BD

London Country:
Lesbourne Road
Reigate
Surrey   RH2 7LE

Orpington and District:
7 Mosyer Drive
Orpington
Kent   BR5 4PN

Maidstone and District:
Opera House Buildings
Tunbridge Wells
Kent

Southdown:
Southdown House
Freshfield Road
Brighton
Sussex   BN2 2BW

Recommended Further Reading

The following list is offered to those who would like to gain more background information on the country through which these two routes lead. It is no way intended to be a comprehensive bibliography, but simply a few suggestions to point the way. Browsing through most public libraries will add to your list, should you be interested.

	The Vanguard Way (Vanguards Rambling Club 1980)
	The Wealdway Long Distance Footpath (Wealdway Steering Group 1981)
Christian, G.	*Ashdown Forest* (Society of Friends of Ashdown Forest 1967)
Cleland, J.	*The Visitor's Guide to Sussex* (Moorland Publishing Co. 1985)
Kaye-Smith, S.	*Weald of Kent and Sussex* (Hale 1973)
Margary, I.D.	*Roman Ways in the Weald* (Dent 1948)
Mason, O.	*South-East England* (Bartholomew 1979)
Mee, A.	*The King's England - Kent* (Hodder & Stoughton 1969)
	The King's England - Sussex (Hodder & Stoughton 1969)
Nair, I.	*Sussex - The Buildings of England Series*, Pevsner, N. (ed.) (Penguin 1973)
Newman, J.	*West Kent and The Weald - The Buildings of England Series*, Pevsner, N. (ed.) (Penguin 1976)
Reynolds, K.	*The Visitor's Guide to Kent* (Moorland Publishing Co. 1985)
Scholes, R.	*Understanding the Countryside* Moorland Publishing Co. 1985
Spence, K.	*The Companion Guide to Kent and Sussex* (Collins 1973)
Straker, E.	*Wealden Iron* (David & Charles 1969)

National Register of Long Distance Paths

A National Register has been established recording details of all the LDP's in Britain. It provides a consultative service for all those concerned with the development of such paths - avoiding duplication of routes, worn paths etc. Please contact the Register at an early stage if you are planning a new route:

National Register of Long Distance Footpaths,
8 Upton Grey Close, Winchester, Hants SO22 6NE.

Printed by Carnmor Print & Design,
95/97, London Road, Preston, Lancashire.